I0560831

Spiritual Leadership

Developing Qualities Worth Following

Michael Fontcnot

www.ipibooks.com

ISBN: 978-1-958723-30-2. Published by Illumination Publishers International.

Unless otherwise indicated, all Scripture references are from the *Holy Bible, New International Version,* copyright ©1973, 1978, 1984, 2011 by Biblica, Inc. Used by permission. All rights reserved worldwide.

Scripture references marked ESV are from *The Holy Bible, English Standard Version.* ESV® Text Edition: 2016. Copyright © 2001 by Crossway Bibles, a publishing ministry of Good News Publishers. References marked TDNT are from the *Theological Dictionary of the New Testament* (10 vols.) by Gerhard Kittel; Geoffrey William Bromiley; Gerhard Friedrich (Eerdmans, 1964).

Interior book design: Toney C. Mulhollan. Cover design by Roy Appalsamy of Toronto, Canada.

Illumination Publishers cares deeply about using renewable resources and uses recycled paper whenever possible. Our titles may be purchased in bulk for classroom instruction, business, fundraising, or sales promotional use. For additional information, please email toneyipibooks@mac.com.

About the author: A graduate of Louisiana State Univiversity, with an MDiv from Fuller Theological Seminary, Mike Fontenot served in the full-time ministry for forty-seven years. In 1981, Mike and Teresa, with their three children, planted a church in Sydney, Australia. They subsequently planted other  churches in Australia and in New Zealand, Fiji, and Papua New Guinea. Mike has served in the USA, Australia, and the UK as an evangelist and an elder. In addition, he served in various global leadership roles through the years. Mike and Teresa are now retired and live in Perth, Australia.

www.ipibooks.com **ILLUMINATION PUBLISHERS**

Contents

Dedication

I would like to dedicate this book to my wife, Tess, of fifty-one years, my three daughters and sons-in-law—Forest and Mandy Versele, Megan and David Bliley, and Sam and Michelle Cameron—and our ten grandchildren. I also greatly appreciate the many brothers and sisters who have served faithfully with us over the last half century and with whom we have learned together the principles in this book.

Foreword

Leadership in God's church will always prove difficult, for two big reasons: Its members all started out as sinners, and its leaders all started out as sinners. Nonetheless, Jesus redeemed each of us with his own blood and sent us his Spirit to collectively transform us into his very image. And so, together, we navigate a holy calling through an unholy world. Throughout the voyage, a siren call continually seeks to seduce us toward the path of Self. The sound is sweet; the argument is "fine-sounding." A small shift to the tiller, and we effortlessly sail toward greater self-satisfaction. But Jesus knows that such a course will dash us upon the rocks. We know it too; he's made it plain to us:

> And he died for all, that those who live should no longer live for themselves but for him who died for them and was raised again. (2 Corinthians 5:15)

> "Whoever wants to be my disciple must deny themselves and take up their cross and follow me. For whoever wants to save their life will lose it, but whoever loses their life for me and for the gospel will save it." (Mark 8:34–35)

> You are not your own; you were bought at a price. (1 Corinthians 6:19b–20a)

> Some people, eager for money, have wandered from the faith and pierced themselves with many griefs. (1 Timothy 6:10b)

If leaders in Jesus' church take his word seriously, we will continually offer ourselves as a countervailing constraint against a culture of ever-increasing consumerism and individualism. As we navigate these complexities, it is essential to ground our leadership in the timeless truths of the gospel. But that's going to take a whole lot of love and courage. This book aims to equip you with the scriptural conviction and practical tools necessary to lead with grace, humility, and clarity. The church needs more servant leaders—for youth groups, small groups, family dynamics, ministry staff, diaconates, and elderships. Anyone aspiring to this noble service will find vital truths for your call in these pages.

As you embark on this journey through the principles and practices of effective church leadership, remember that you are part of a larger story—one that spans generations and is written by the hands of countless faithful servants before you. Their legacy, and now yours, is to uphold the integrity of the church, to preach the gospel with clarity and conviction, and to shepherd God's people with love and diligence.

Mike Fontenot is uniquely fit for this task. He has weathered storms yet remains steadfast, refusing to be "tossed back and forth by the waves, and blown here and there by every wind of teaching." As Mike has held fast to the word of truth, he has helped generations of leaders on every inhabited continent to do the same. I count myself among them. He taught me to love Jesus, love his word, and love his church.

May this book inspire you, equip you, and remind you of the high calling you have received. As we turn the pages together, let us recommit ourselves to lead with the passion of Peter, the focus of Paul, and the servant heart of Jesus Christ.

—Ed Anton
Evangelist and Teacher

Introduction

As each has received a gift, use it to serve one another, as good stewards of God's varied grace: whoever speaks, as one who speaks oracles of God; whoever serves, as one who serves by the strength that God supplies—in order that in everything God may be glorified through Jesus Christ. To him belong glory and dominion forever and ever. Amen. (1 Peter 4:10–11)

Having gifts that differ according to the grace given to us, let us use them: if prophecy, in proportion to our faith; if service, in our serving; the one who teaches, in his teaching; the one who exhorts, in his exhortation; the one who contributes, in generosity; the one who leads, with zeal; the one who does acts of mercy, with cheerfulness. (Romans 12:6–8 ESV)

During a leadership training program, I had a conversation with two university students. I asked if they were interested in the full-time ministry after they graduated.

Both were great young men. The first said he was about ten percent interested, and the other responded that he was fifteen percent interested. This response did not sit well with me for several reasons.

First, if one is gifted in leadership, the Scriptures are clear that we are meant to use whatever gift we were given to serve God's people. One needs to ask others if they are gifted, for it is not just one's personal opinion about themselves that matters; they should ask others if perhaps God has gifted them to serve in leadership. We all need to be one hundred percent interested to serve God in whatever way and with however we are gifted that is useful for him for the good of the body of Christ.

Second, everyone needs to be reminded of some key scriptures.

> I know, O LORD, that the way of man is not in himself,
> that it is not in man who walks to direct his steps. (Jeremiah 10:23 ESV)

> Or do you not know that your body is a temple of the Holy Spirit within you, whom you have from God? You are not your own, for you were bought with a price. So glorify God in your body. (1 Corinthians 6:19–20 ESV)

> You were bought with a price; do not become bondservants of men. (1 Corinthians 7:23 ESV)

> But false prophets also arose among the people, just as there will be false teachers among you, who will secretly bring in destructive heresies, even denying the Master who bought them, bringing upon themselves swift destruction. (2 Peter 2:1 ESV)

> I have been crucified with Christ. It is no longer I who live, but Christ who lives in me. And the life I now live in the flesh I live by faith in the Son of God, who loved me and gave himself for me. (Galatians 2:20 ESV)

In a culture where more than 30 percent in Italy and 20 percent in the rest of the empire on average were slaves, everyone understood what being bought meant. There were slave markets throughout the Roman Empire where slaves stood on platforms with a plaque hung around their necks describing their health, skills, intelligence, and education. They were purchased for various functions for their owner—for if bought, then owned. What is the chance that a slave being purchased for a certain function would tell his buyer and new master that they were ten percent interested in serving in that capacity? Sorry, sir, not sure I want to serve in that function; let me think about. It is not part of my plan for my life.

Yet in our present culture, most approach their discipleship with this attitude. We listen to and wink at what it means to give up all and follow Jesus—he doesn't really mean it; it's just metaphorical language. But it really isn't. It is a narrow door and a narrow road. And it does mean something.

Slaves were often freed, but more often they were sold to other masters. This seems to be part of the language here. We were slaves to sin, but now are slaves to Christ (Romans 6). We were all slaves, not based on race, but on our actions and character.

But the purchase is also described in 1 Peter 1:18-19: "You were ransomed from the futile ways inherited from your forefathers, not with perishable things such as silver or gold, but with the precious blood of Christ, like that of a lamb without blemish or spot" (ESV).

Not everyone by any means needs to lead in the full-time ministry. But we all likely will find ourselves in a position where our Master expects spiritual leadership. As parents, husbands, discussion group leaders, or helping a young disciple mature in their faith in Jesus, we all have leadership roles. Whether we like it or not is not the question. The question is not how Jesus can serve me, but how does Jesus, my master, want me to serve.

One of the marks of false teachers and their teaching is described in the following scriptures:

> But false prophets also arose among the people, just as there will be false teachers among you, who will secretly bring in destructive heresies, even denying the Master who bought them, bringing upon themselves swift destruction. (2 Peter 2:1 ESV)

> For certain people have crept in unnoticed who long ago were designated for this condemnation, ungodly people, who pervert the grace of our God into sensuality and deny our only Master and Lord, Jesus Christ. (Jude 4 ESV)

These epistles are considered to have been written toward the end of the apostolic age and addressed to those who had been disciples for a while. Many of us started our discipleship in our idealistic youth. But then after many years of following Jesus, with our careers and families, our personal expectations of discipleship have gotten watered down by life. Even in the New Testament, the same pattern seemed to have occurred. "Jesus is Lord" means something. The false teachers watered down his sovereignty and his role as Master and Lord. They perverted the grace of God into a license to do whatever one wants, not considering what God wants. It is not just a characteristic of our culture, but of every culture.

I became a disciple when I was nineteen. My life was that of a typical fraternity guy attending a university known for its party life. Then I switched to a student gathering filled mainly with students who were raised in the church and never went off to the "world." I was bewildered by their lack of passion and enthusiasm. They talked of discovering the grace of God and having been governed by the rules of the church (legalism). They responded to me with the notion that they were different. They weren't worldly sinners who repented, so their expressions of faith were less dramatic.

Biblically speaking, to them I was the prodigal son, but they were the older brother. They were Simon the Pharisee (Luke 7), and I was the sinful woman washing Jesus' feet because her sins were forgiven. What they didn't realize was that in fact, they were just as big a sinner as I was, but they could not see their sins because their sins were "respectable" ones. Arrogance, pride, judgmentalism, deceitfulness, and many more could be named. These are the sins of the religious folk. Jesus could exorcise the most heinous demon and send it into the abyss with just one word. With a thousand words, he barely put a dent in those with a religious spirit.

But how I started does not mean that the religious spirit has not crept into my life as I have aged. There is something about our sinful nature that even though we may live in a glorious place (I live in Perth, and it is beautiful), after a while, we no longer see what others come as tourists to behold. So it is with our faith.

God's church needs great spiritual leadership to revive it to a fresh state of extreme thanksgiving about God and the lives he has redeemed and bought. It is time, if you haven't been in the game, to get back in and stop sitting in the stands critiquing the team and arrogantly thinking you could do better. Well, get dressed and get back in. If your gift is leading, then lead with zeal.

Those two uni students mentioned earlier, by the way, are now in the full-time ministry, and their comments continue to offer a humorous teaching lesson to others.

· Chapter One ·

Servant Leadership: A Given

> Jesus called them together and said, "You know that the rulers of the Gentiles lord it over them, and their high officials exercise authority over them. Not so with you. Instead, whoever wants to become great among you must be your servant, and whoever wants to be first must be your slave—just as the Son of Man did not come to be served, but to serve, and to give his life as a ransom for many." (Matthew 20:25–28)

Jesus made it perfectly clear that those who would be great, who would be first, must not lead like those in the world.

He does not dismiss their ambition as being the core problem. He has called those who follow him with the challenge to change the world—to be fishers of men, to go into the ends of the earth and bear witness of what Jesus has done to save us. The disciple of Jesus is no sweet, passive, religious individual as personified in so many literary and film caricatures. He is not docile. Jesus' call to his first disciples was not a passive call. It was not, "Come follow me and have a personal relationship with me." How strange that would have sounded to those manly fishermen! It was an invitation to impact the whole planet. (Yes, they would develop a personal relationship with Jesus—but that is a product of that call. They were to be with him.)

But their ambition was meant to be governed by spirituality, not just a personality type. They were trained to be servants to others, not to have others serve them. And the service could include the lowliest of tasks. Too many times, ambitious people are placed in leadership without their spirituality being tested first and foremost. And though Jesus taught his disciples this servanthood, he also demonstrated it. It did not automatically sink in, but was a lesson repeated numerous times and in every gospel.

We do lead from the front. But unlike the world, our charge is to not "lord it over" those we lead but to be a servant to them. "To lord over" is the Greek word *katakyrieúō*. Although the force of *katá* (over) is mostly lost in ordinary usage, it conveys the sense of rule to one's own advantage seen in Mark 10:42 (Gentile rulers), Acts 19:16 (the evil spirit), and 1 Peter 5:2-3 (the admonition to the elders not to lord it over).

In other words, to serve is to put others' interests above our own. That is a rare person. When Paul commends Timothy to the Philippians, he commends him for his selfless attitude: "I have no one else like him, who will show genuine concern for your welfare. For everyone looks out for their own interests, not those of Jesus Christ" (Philippians 2:20-21). I have no one else like him! Really! No one. It was a rare person even for Paul, who had contact with some pretty awesome saints. It is still a rare quality found in leaders.

Paul in this same chapter has highlighted the Christlike attitude we are all meant to have: "Do nothing out of selfish ambition or vain conceit. Rather, in humility value others above yourselves, not looking to your own interests but each of you to the interests of the others" (vv. 3-4). This is based on our Lord's example, making himself nothing for the sake of our salvation. Not what was good for him, but what was necessary for our salvation—even to the point of a painful death for our good.

Godly leaders count others as more significant than themselves. Worldly leaders value themselves as the most significant and teach others to give them the most significance. Others don't come to do the work of godly leaders, who regularly help others with their work.

It is very difficult to keep your head straight when so many things about leadership can puff one up. There is the constant encouragement, sometimes flattery, and the internal thrill one feels when engaged in preaching or teaching, all of which can inflate one, or puff one up. Paul uses this language in 1 Corinthians 4:6-7:

> I have applied all these things to myself and Apollos for your benefit, brothers, that you may learn by us not to go beyond what is written, that none of you may be *puffed* up in favor of one against another. For who sees anything different in you? What do you have that you did not receive? If then you received it, why do you boast as if you did not receive it? (ESV, emphasis added).

"Puffed up," φυσιόω *phusioo*, is used in the primary sense of blowing; to inflate, i.e., (figuratively) make proud (haughty): puff up (*Strong's Greek Dictionary*). It is an onomatopoeia, sounding like what it means, just like our word "puffed." We get full of ourselves. Narcissists are often attracted to leadership—we see it in all walks of life.

Jesus ran from those who would force him to be king because they were impressed with the feeding of the 5,000. This was another temptation of worldly leadership without sacrifice, of a Christ without the cross, another "opportune time" when Satan tempted Jesus.

As Paul writes in Philippians 2:7 of the example of Jesus:

> ...rather, he made himself nothing
> by taking the very nature of a servant,...

> ...but emptied himself, by taking the form of a servant,... ESV

Much has been written concerning what it meant for Jesus to make himself nothing. Profound theological truths are considered about Jesus being truly God and truly man at the same time and how this fits into this concept. The purpose of this book is not to address that.

The Greek word *kenos*, κενός *kenós* [empty], κενόω *kenóō* [to make empty], is the word translated as making oneself nothing (TDNT).

If the example is given so that we can imitate Christ, what does it mean for us to make ourselves nothing? To empty ourselves! That is the purpose Paul writes to them about and for us to consider. What are some tests of our heart and actions regarding this?

1. Have I rationalized my leadership as my service? I serve my people in leading, counseling, discipling—so they can serve me in the menial tasks of life. I am the "benefactor"; I give my leadership, and they clean my house. I give my counseling, and they do garden work for me. The Greek benefactor gave, but he gave with expectations of those given to, to show their gratitude. There is a biblical truth that the "worker deserves his wages." But there is also the biblical truth of Jesus' style of leadership that stoops to washing feet. Is your conscience sensitive to applying servanthood to your ministry? Was David's response to those who overheard his longing for some sweet Bethlehem water, "Thanks, bros, for serving"? There is nothing wrong with delegating the many needs of service to others in leadership. But there must also be a deliberate effort to anonymously serve God's people in what might be regarded as humble ways.

2. If I claim to have made myself nothing, how do I feel when I do not get credit and recognition for my service while others do? How do I feel when I am not mentioned in sermons for my service while others are?

3. How do I feel when I step back in some roles of leadership because of age, health, or family issues and no one seems interested in my acute insights and (self-pro-

claimed) wisdom? This is especially true of those who are moving into retirement.

4. How selfless am I in putting others' interests above my own? How willing am I to help another ministry at the expense of weakening mine? I won't share with others if it reduces my own success.

5. Do I always prioritize time with those who can help me at conferences while not having time for those who need help?

· Chapter Two ·

Clothed in Humility

"Come to me, all you who are weary and burdened, and I will give you rest. Take my yoke upon you and learn from me, for I am gentle and humble in heart, and you will find rest for your souls. For my yoke is easy and my burden is light." (Matthew 11:28–30)

Now Moses was a very humble man, more humble than anyone else on the face of the earth. (Numbers 12:3)

The great invitation of Jesus is to take his yoke upon us, for he is gentle and humble in heart. If we have accepted that invitation and decided to be his disciple, humility should be a hallmark of our lives as well. The student is not above his teacher: "A disciple is not above his teacher, nor a servant above his master. It is enough for the disciple to be like his teacher, and the servant like his master" (Matthew 10:24–25a ESV). We are meant to be like him, humble and gentle.

Leadership always carries with it the temptation to pride. We want to do great things for God, and we pray to God to be used to do great things with his help. Yet despite our prayer and intellectual agreement that it is due to God and his help, we quickly devolve into the notion that it was really about us. Why is my ministry growing and some others are not? It's the same God, isn't it, so it must be about me. And there is truth in that. There has to be. But the reason is not who we are with all our "gifts" and talents, but our faith and dependance on God and his word.

We see this repeated in the Old Testament time and time again. Let's look at a few examples.

Moses

Moses was described as a very humble man. It is impressive to read about his life and faith. It is amazing that, when the people grumble and complain, and God is ready to end them all and start over with Moses alone, Moses pleads with God not to abandon his people (Numbers 14:11-14). When Miriam criticizes Moses for marrying a Cushite woman, God strikes her with leprosy, and Moses pleads with the Lord for her healing (Numbers 12:13). This pattern continues until the second incident with the rock bringing forth water, when Moses strikes the rock instead of following the exact instructions God had given him to speak to it. But what stands out more than the specific disobedience to God's instruction is how Moses' attitude toward the people that he has been serving has changed. Numbers 20:9-12 says:

> So Moses took the staff from the LORD'S presence, just as he commanded him. He and Aaron gathered the assembly together in front of the rock and Moses said to them, "Listen, you rebels, must we bring you water out of this rock?" Then Moses raised his arm and struck the rock twice with his staff. Water gushed out, and the community and their livestock drank.
>
> But the LORD said to Moses and Aaron, "Because you did not trust in me enough to honor me as holy in the sight of the Israelites, you will not bring this community into the land I give them."

No longer is Moses pleading with God to be gracious despite their lack of faith and grumbling; he now addresses them as "rebels." Even as Moses at the end of his life is making his recollection of all that has happened, he is still blaming the people rather than being humble about himself and his change of heart as God's leader.

> At that time I pleaded with the LORD: "Sovereign LORD, you have begun to show to your servant your greatness and your strong hand. For what god is there in heaven or on earth who can do the deeds and mighty works you do? Let me go over and see the good land beyond the Jordan—that fine hill country and Lebanon."
>
> But because of you the LORD was angry with me and would not listen to me. "That is enough," the LORD said. "Do not speak to me anymore about this matter." (Deuteronomy 3:23:23–26)

In other words, the Lord says, "Shut up, Moses. Enough is enough! You no longer have a heart for the people. You have forgotten about putting your people above yourself. Now it is all about how they are treating you!" Moses, like Elijah, at the end of his ministry has lost his love for the people and fails to see his own heart. God says, enough of that, Moses, much like he says to Elijah, who complains about the people and says that only he alone is standing for the truth. (What about the other seven thousand who have not bowed the knee to Baal?)

> "What are you doing here, Elijah?"
>
> "He replied, "I have been very zealous for the LORD God Almighty. The Israelites have rejected your covenant, torn down your altars, and put your prophets to death with the sword. I am the only one left, and now they are trying to kill me too." (1 Kings 19:9–10)

And so God says to Elijah basically the same: "Enough, Elijah, I have tried to get you to see—the wind, earthquake, and fire, and then the low whisper. It is time for you to move on. Get ready to anoint your replacement." Humility is not expressed as life being all about me and not God! It is essential to continue as Jesus did and empty himself for the sake of others. That is humility.

David

Stephen states in Acts 13:22: "After removing Saul, he made David their king. God testified concerning him: 'I have found David son of Jesse, a man after my own heart; he will do everything I want him to do.'" Following a list of all David's victories in 2 Samuel 10, starting in chapter 11:1 where it describes the season, the springtime when kings go to battle, it says David stays home. What follows is spiritual disaster with Bathsheba and her husband. What follows is adultery and murder.

> The crucible for silver and the furnace for gold,
>> but people are tested by their praise. (Proverbs 27:21)

David will be tested and fail. The praise is there. The victories are there! But so is the temptation to pride. Even in the difficult chapter at the end of 2 Samuel, when David decides to count the fighting men even over the objection of Joab (when Joab is more righteous than David, you know there is going to be trouble), there seems to be an issue of pride. It is commanded to take such a census in Exodus 30:12, but it must be done properly. It is also commanded in Numbers 1:2; 4:2, 22; and 26:2. One possible interpretation of many is that the sin was taking a census for his own self-exaltation of his military powers and prowess rather than trusting in God. There is nothing wrong with stats used in a healthy way, but something is very unhealthy when they are used for our glory and boasting.

Uzziah

But after Uzziah became powerful, his pride led to his downfall. He was unfaithful to the LORD his God, and entered the temple of the LORD to burn incense on the altar of incense. Azariah the priest with eighty other courageous priests of the LORD followed him in. They confronted King Uzziah and said, "It is not right for you, Uzziah, to burn incense to the LORD. That is for the priests, the descendants of Aaron, who have been consecrated to burn incense. Leave the sanctuary, for you have been unfaithful; and you will not be honored by the LORD God."

Uzziah, who had a censer in his hand ready to burn incense, became angry. While he was raging at the priests in their presence before the incense altar in the LORD'S temple, leprosy broke out on his forehead. When Azariah the chief priest and all the other priests looked at him, they saw that he had leprosy on his fore-head, so they hurried him out. Indeed, he himself was eager to leave, because the LORD had afflicted him. (2 Chronicles 26:16–20)

The great king thus collapses when he is above humbly following God's specific commands, even what some might regard as insignificant rules.

Hezekiah

In those days Hezekiah became ill and was at the point of death. He prayed to the LORD, who answered him and gave him a miraculous sign. But Hezekiah's heart was proud and he did not respond to the kind-ness shown him; therefore the LORD'S wrath was on him and on Judah and Jerusalem. Then Hezekiah re-pented of the pride of his heart, as did the people of Jerusalem; therefore the LORD'S wrath did not come on them during the days of Hezekiah. (2 Chronicles 32:24–26; cf. King Asa in 2 Chronicles 16:12)

It is a common problem. If it was a problem for them, it will be a problem for us. Arrogance is a more recognizable sin than its sister pride. Arrogance is on the surface, but pride can be hidden in one's heart. Arrogance is typical in young leaders, who in their idealism expect everything to flow smoothly. "We'll have no seri-ous problems in our marriages and families. How could we with

God on our side, and we are his people? We are different from everybody else." It is as if thinking since we have right doctrine in crucial areas, this will protect us. But the real issue is the sin of pride and arrogance. As time goes by, our confidence in ourselves and our commitment to Jesus leaks away, and like the salt from the Dead Sea that is mixed with impurities, over time the salt disappears, leaving something that looks like salt but that has lost its taste and influence. We then move to a defensive posture lest our true self come out. We become overly sensitive to any criticism. We are absorbed and worried about losing our position rather than what is best for the church. So we have a need to boast to convince others and even ourselves that we are God's spiritual leaders. We have slipped from grace, that our salvation is all from Christ's death on the cross, and now it is more about our performance. As Paul says in Romans 3, if we understand grace and atonement, how can we ever boast!

How many times have I sabotaged a good plan by boasting of the plan itself as if the plan were the crucial element, not our faith in God?

In contrast, we can look at Joseph. Though the text does not say it, I believe it is implied that as a young man having visions that were centered on him, he had no problem telling his brothers and parents of those visions. It is hard to believe that the clever young Joseph wasn't aware of what the vision meant of having his brothers and parents bowing to him. Did he have no clue that wearing the flashy coat would set his brothers off?

Yet God, through all that happened to him in family betrayal, slavery, and prison, forged Joseph into a pure instrument to save his people. At the end, when Joseph sits high and mighty, he tells his brothers in tears as they fear retribution, that all that had happened was God's plan for the salvation of many. It is not about him; it is all about God's people.

What are some things to consider to be the humble leaders that God desires?

- Always plan to be in a ministry that requires more faith. That usually means being open to moving and revitalizing not only the new ministry but yourself as well. The very nature of staying put can tempt us to hold onto something rather than trusting God with our future, especially as we age. Everyone can and will get stale and flat. As is said proverbially, "A change is as good as a holiday." But don't just refresh yourself, refresh the local church with new, fresh leadership. This need doesn't change when we get older and more sedentary. Abraham had his greatest challenge put to him in the call to sacrifice his son, Issac, the one he loved, at the end of his story, his journey.

- Leadership is by nature lonely at times. One must have a group of brothers or sisters who ask the right questions of us, people who really know us. I have found that we need both local people and others outside our local ministry to be around us to give us fresh input to keep us from being deceived by sin's deceitfulness.

Take care, brothers, lest there be in any of you an evil, unbelieving heart, leading you to fall away from the living God. But exhort one another every day, as long as it is called "today," that none of you may be hardened by the deceitfulness of sin. For we have come to share in Christ, if indeed we hold our original confidence firm to the end. As it is said,
"Today, if you hear his voice,
do not harden your hearts as in the rebellion." Hebrews 3:12–15 ESV

These verses sound like a healthy discipleship or accountability group. Did David mess up because there was no longer a Jonathan in his life? Don't ever expect all the input to come from people you lead. It just doesn't naturally work that way.

- Make sure you keep part of your schedule on the grassroots level of the ministry. If we are involved in studying the Bible with unbelievers, it keeps us fresh and connected to the real needs of people. Studying sin with someone and sharing your life and the sins that you have repented of and still struggle with definitely massages your heart in the right way and reminds us of our need for grace and thankfulness.

- Purposely involve others in your ministry and ask for their appraisal of your ministry. Don't wait to be told, but constantly initiate with every visiting leader asking for their "out of the box" perspective. Invite others in as often as possible to help refine your service to God. Take extra initiative about your marriage and family, the very areas we get the most defensive about, especially our children.

· Chapter Three ·

Faithful Leadership

"'If you can'?" said Jesus. "Everything is possible for one who believes."Immediately the boy's father exclaimed, "I do believe; help me overcome my unbelief!" (Mark 9:23-24)

Then the disciples came to Jesus in private and asked, "Why couldn't we drive it out?"He replied, "Because you have so little faith. Truly I tell you, if you have faith as small as a mustard seed, you can say to this mountain, 'Move from here to there,' and it will move. Nothing will be impossible for you." (Matthew 17:19-20)

As Jesus went on from there, two blind men followed him, calling out, "Have mercy on us, Son of David!"
When he had gone indoors, the blind men came to him, and he asked them, "Do you believe that I am able to do this?""Yes, Lord," they replied.Then he touched their eyes and said, "According to your faith let it be done to you." (Matthew 9:27-29)

Over the years, there have been many new programs presented as the "silver bullet" way to help and to grow the church. It could have been busing children to Sunday school on a "Joy Bus," a marriage series designed to make everyone happily married, a new form of evangelism (Bible talks), a study series that would equip everyone, or a new spiritual horoscope describing everyone in the church as a certain personality type (the Greeks did the same thing over two thousand years ago), or everyone figuring out their spiritual gift and living happily ever after in fulfilled lives with less angst about the commandments they might be avoiding.

These were presented with zeal by successful promoters of their program. Many were great ideas, but programs don't move the church, faith does. And without that faith, most churches just move from one program to the next flavor-of-the-year method. You can't put on Saul's armor and expect to beat Goliath.

Let's consider a couple of scriptures about faithful leadership. There are so many to choose from!

The first follows the transfiguration of Jesus on the high mountain with Peter, James, and John. There are several big takeaways from that moment, but for sure, listening to Jesus is the main one (the Law and the Prophets point to Jesus—Moses and Elijah). They come down from the mountain and find the other nine apostles involved in a verbal brawl with the disciples, surrounded by a crowd and with the teachers of the law arguing with them. The issue is that a boy was brought with a severe case of demonic possession, and the nine disciples who had remained had not been able to cast it out. Jesus deals dramatically with the boy. According to Jesus, it is not just his absence from them at that moment, but chiefly, their lack of faith in him that made them ineffective. They have a lack of faith in Jesus, since if they had even a mustard seed worth, there would not have been a problem. They fell back to a defensive position based on their ability. The father responded in Mark 9:18, "I asked your disciples to drive out the spirit, but they could not." They could not! We will come back to that point later in this chapter. They, like so many of us, under pressure, went from faith to self-reliance, crumbling in the process.

The father of the boy is also struggling with his faith. Nothing has worked, and Jesus' disciples have not come through. When the father asks Jesus in the form of a request with subtle doubt, "If you can do anything, have compassion on us and help us"

(Mark 9:22 ESV), Jesus challenges him. "If you can," if you have any compassion, if you can help, implies to Jesus that this father has a faith problem.

Faithful leaders can move mountains. All things are possible for faithful disciples and faithful leaders. These words are powerful and inspiring and at the same time confusing to us when we face trials in our leadership and have obstacles galore in our way. There can be problems both without and within that make our prayer life sound like "Father, please, oh Lord, if you can, please help us here."

Certain problems can be flaming arrows shot at our shield of faith (Ephesians 6:16) that slip through like a sucker punch to our gut. Problems like:

- Will this disciple of Jesus really ever change?
- Can this grumpy person in my ministry ever stop being critical about everything?
- Can my children get along, come to faith, handle the world at school?
- Can my ministry grow?
- Can we find some open people who want to become Christians?
- Can we change the atmosphere of the church to become a faithful, joyful group of disciples?

We can start to think things like, *"If only I had a better group of people to work with (like someone's else group), then I could really move the ministry forward and save souls and keep them saved."*

The other pericope to glean some teaching on faithfulness involves the two blind men who approach Jesus in Matthew 9:27ff. The context involves Jesus healing a woman suffering for twelve years who, seemingly out of embarrassment due to uncleanness, secretly touches the fringe of Jesus' garment and is healed, just as he is traveling with Jarius, whose daughter has died. Jesus has challenged him not to give in to fear but to continue to believe in the face of death itself (see also Mark 5:36). Word was spreading rapidly, as would be expected. As he passes on from there, two blind men are following him, crying loudly and begging Jesus, whom they address as the Son of David, to have mercy on them. In Matthew 9:28 Jesus does what we don't expect while these two men are screaming: He enters the house he was going to. The scene is striking in that it seems Jesus just ignores them. They are blind and thus oblivious to the fact that Jesus has left the road and entered the house. One could think this was cold. They beg for mercy, he ignores them, and goes indoors. Jesus is looking for faith. But faith shines out in desperate circumstances!

The two blind men could have given up. They could have become discouraged and doubted that God really wanted to help them. They could have doubted that Jesus was really the Son of David (a very messianic idiom) because of his cold response. They could have resigned themselves to their fate and given up hope of changing the course of their lives. They could have just comforted one another to be accepting of their situation. Yet, obviously, that is not the conversation that they had. They instead must have said, "We have already been making fools of ourselves; let's not give up now." And, apparently being directed by others, they enter the house Jesus is in and approach him.

Jesus knows what they want. That is not his question to them. But he does ask quite a remarkable question: *"Do you believe that I am able to do this"?* (Matthew 9:28). It is a very specific question that addresses their faith. But it is not just about faith in faith. Too many times we think of faith as something we have to generate within ourselves. *"If I could just have more faith,"* we think, as if the quality of faith would make all the difference. Even though we have in the back of our mind that quantity is never the issue (remember the mustard-seed mountain-moving faith), we think we need to be like the little train engine that is talking to itself with positive thinking, *If I can just believe in myself, I can get over this hill—I think I can! I think I can! I think I can!* We think faith is about plenty of optimism and some hard work.

But Jesus does not ask them to generate faith in themselves. He asks if they think he is able. It is all about their focus of faith, and that focus must be Jesus. Again, Jesus asks, do you think *I am able?*

There was a time while in university that I transferred from LSU to the University of Missouri in St. Louis to be part of a growing ministry. It is over six hundred miles north of LSU. That was going to be a major change in weather. I moved in the middle of winter. Growing up in the Deep South in the US, I had never experienced truly cold weather. Behind my apartment was a lake that, to my wonder, was frozen. I had never seen or experienced a frozen lake down in Louisiana. So one afternoon I went down to the lake to try my hand at walking on water! There was no one around or on the lake. I was very nervous, worried that I would fall through the ice and be lost until the Spring thaw. Nevertheless, I ventured out toward the middle, walking on my tiptoes, knowing we weigh less if we tippy toe. I bravely moved out and nervously made my way back to the shore. After I got there, up walked two high school guys who put on their skates and with their hockey sticks boldly skated around the lake. They had no worries; they were simply enjoying the experience.

Now here's the question: Who was safest? Were they safer than I was? The answer of course was that we were equally safe. The reason is that it wasn't my little faith in the ice nor their confidence in the ice that changed our safety. It wasn't our attitude that kept us from crashing through the ice, it was the strength and thickness of the ice that mattered.

So, when Jesus asked the question whether they believed he was able, it was not about their attitude in themselves, but their attitude toward him. Was he able? If we can focus on that, with faith even as small as a mustard seed, great, unimaginable things can happen.

You might ask, "What is the difference between little faith and great faith?" I think the difference is seen in the quality of our spiritual life. I was fearful, doubtful, worried, stressed, and thinking about the worst thing that could happen. They were, in contrast, really enjoying life.

And of course, because they had great faith in the ice, they did remarkable things on their skates. I did very little in fear of what might go wrong. I avoided movement; they embraced it.

Our faith, then, will influence all that we might do for God. Jesus responds to the blind men by touching their eyes and saying, "According to your faith let it be done to you"; and their sight was restored (Matthew 9:29–30).

Let's now examine some illustrations of this in the Old Testament.

First, in 2 Kings 4:1–7:

> Now the wife of one of the sons of the prophets cried to Elisha, "Your servant my husband is dead, and you know that your servant feared the LORD, but the creditor has come to take my two children to be his slaves." And Elisha said to her, "What shall I do for you? Tell me; what have you in the house?" And she said, "Your servant has nothing in the house except a jar of oil." Then he said, "Go outside, borrow vessels from all your neighbors, empty vessels and not too few. Then go in and shut the door behind yourself and your sons and pour into all these vessels. And when one is full, set it aside." So she went from him and shut the door behind herself and her sons. And as she poured they brought the vessels to her. When the vessels were full, she said to her son, "Bring me another vessel." And he said to her, "There is not another." Then the oil stopped flowing. She came and told the man of God, and he said, "Go, sell the oil and pay your debts, and you and your sons can live on the rest." (ESV)

Elisha is approached by the widow of one of the prophets. She had two young sons and, having no safety net for such circumstances, was in danger of having her two children sold into slavery. One can only imagine the distress she felt. Elisha asks how he can help. "What do you have in your house?" "Nothing! Just one jar of oil." He tells her to go around the village and borrow as many empty jars as she can and not to be shy about the number. The story is clear about what happens. The question is this: If she gathered ten jars, how much oil would she have? Ten jars full. What if she gathered one thousand jars? How much oil would she have? I believe she would have had one thousand jars of oil. So her faith would affect the quality of deliverance for her and her sons. How much are we expecting in our ministry?

Let's consider another incident in 2 Kings 13:14–20:

> Now Elisha had been suffering from the illness from which he died. Jehoash king of Israel went down to see him and wept over him. "My father! My father!" he cried. "The chariots and horsemen of Israel!"
>
> Elisha said, "Get a bow and some arrows," and he did so. "Take the bow in your hands," he said to the king of Israel. When he had taken it, Elisha put his hands on the king's hands.
>
> "Open the east window," he said, and he opened it. "Shoot!" Elisha said, and he shot. "The LORD'S arrow of victory, the arrow of victory over Aram (Syria)!" Elisha declared. "You will completely destroy the Arameans at Aphek."
>
> Then he said, "Take the arrows," and the king took them. Elisha told him, "Strike the ground." He struck it three times and stopped. The man of God was angry with him and said, "You should have struck the ground five or six times; then you would have defeated Aram and completely destroyed it. But now you will defeat it only three times."
>
> Elisha died and was buried.

In a similar way, Jehoash the King of Israel approaches Elisha at his deathbed. He has been involved in a struggle with the country of Aram. Elisha has him shoot an arrow out the window in a joint effort and exclaims, "The Lord's arrow of victory." Then he is told to take the arrows on his own and strike the ground. We don't know what is going on in Jehoash's mind. Does he start to strike the ground and then become self-conscious doing what might seem foolish? Does he become self-absorbed and hesitate so that he only strikes three times? Elisha hints that he does hesitate and becomes angry with him. "Why didn't you strike five or six times?" Why not a hundred times? So, there would only be partial success. It would be according to his faith.

Jesus goes to his hometown of Nazareth, and Mark 6:5-6 records that "he could not do any miracles there, except lay his hands on a few sick people and heal them. He was amazed at their lack of faith." Again, according to their faith, little happened. The problem is not God. The problem involves our focus on Jesus and faith that he is able.

The question is, What is the object of our focus? In this day of self-focus, if you have the mindset that it is all about me, my truth, my feelings, and my injustices, or whatever, do not expect much to happen in your ministry. It is supremely important to spend our time in God's word and in prayer to focus on what is possible with Jesus!

Instead of self-evaluation, spend time in Jesus evaluation and what is possible through him. Don't listen to the whispers of others like those who were in Jarius's ear saying not to bother the teacher any more, since his daughter had died. Imagine all that God can do through your ministry. It is not all about you, but all about him.

And if nothing is happening in your ministry and leadership, don't just turn to the newest ministry flavor of the month, turn to Jesus who can do the impossible.

· Chapter Four ·

If Leading, Then with Zeal

For by the grace given me I say to every one of you: Do not think of yourself more highly than you ought, but rather think of yourself with sober judgment, in accordance with the faith God has distributed to each of you. For just as each of us has one body with many members, and these members do not all have the same function, so in Christ we, though many, form one body, and each member belongs to all the others. We have different gifts, according to the grace given to each of us. If your gift is...to lead, do it diligently. (Romans 12:3–6, 8b)

For by the grace given to me I say to everyone among you not to think of himself more highly than he ought to think, but to think with sober judgment, each according to the measure of faith that God has assigned. For as in one body we have many members, and the members do not all have the same function, so we, though many, are one body in Christ, and individually members one of another. Having gifts that differ according to the grace given to us, let us use them: ... the one who leads, with zeal. (Romans 12:3–6, 8b ESV)

Leadership is gifted leadership, gifted by God to serve his church, his people. It is described in this passage in the original language as ὁ προϊστάμενος ἐν σπουδῇ προΐστημι proístēmi, [to be at the head of, rule, care for] (TDNT). This is a combination of two Greek words, *pro:* "in front of" and *istemi:* "to stand."

The leaders stand in front! They lead from the front. Where I live in Australia, with a sheep population of seventy-eight million, three times our human population, the sheep are driven from the rear with motorcycles and ATVs propelling them forward, and sheep dogs nipping at their heels.

In the Ancient Near East, the shepherd led from the front. Jesus illustrates this often in the Gospels. Mark 10:32 says: "They were on their way up to Jerusalem, with Jesus leading the way, and the disciples were astonished, while those who followed were afraid." They were headed to Jerusalem. Jesus had spoken of trouble ahead, and he leads them right into it.

The second word, translated as "diligence" or "zeal," is σπουδή *spoudé* [haste, zeal], σπουδαῖος *spoudaíos*, "speedy, zealous." From *spoudé* ("haste"), *spoudázō* means "to make haste" or transitively "to hurry something on," then "to treat seriously or respectfully" (TDNT).

There is always a danger in impulsive, reactionary leadership. But there is an equal if not greater danger in leadership that is slow, over-deliberating, and stifling to forward movement.

The most common translation of this word is "haste." Spiritual leadership needs to be proactive. (See other examples in 2 Timothy 4:9, 21; Titus 2:15; Ephesians 4:3.)

"Haste" synonyms are "speed," "hurry," "swiftness," "rapidity," "quickness." It is meant to be decisive. It is leadership as described to disciples "in the battle." It is the spiritual warfare we are meant to be engaged in as Jesus' disciples, wearing the spiritual armor described by Paul in Ephesians 6:11ff. But too often our leadership can look like boardroom committee leadership. There is lots of talk with "action points" language that hardly describes the process.

Our prayer life should be the language of being on the battlefield talking on our walkie-talkie to God with haste in mind. Too often, our prayer life is more akin to sitting in the backyard garden sipping tea than like Jesus in the Garden of Gethsemane preparing for battle.

It is seen in the action of faithful kings in Judah. Josiah hears God's rediscovered word read aloud and immediately takes action—with haste! (2 Chronicles 34).

It is not *seen* in Elijah, who in the end of his ministry is given an assignment to appoint Hazael to be king over Syria, Jehu to be king over Israel, and Elisha to be prophet in his place (1 Kings 19:15-16). He does appoint Elisha, the easiest of the tasks, but the more difficult, especially Jehu, he doesn't get around to. There is an old English myth about King Arthur. In Medieval times, the legendary king had assembled twelve chivalrous knights of the realm to protect the kingdom from evil and harm. King Arthur asked the wizard Merlin to fashion a finely crafted, large round table (known as a Round Tuit) to be used for the assemblage of the twelve knights. Twelve gathered at the round table, no one now was in front. How did that end? It morphed into an English metaphor of jobs that are meant to be done but no one is getting around to it!

Why did Elijah hesitate with Jehu? For Elijah never met with Jehu, and his replacement never got around to it either, that is Elisha. Finally, he sends a message in 2 Kings 9:1-3.

> The prophet Elisha summoned a man from the company of the prophets and said to him, "Tuck your cloak into your belt, take this flask of olive oil with you and go to Ramoth Gilead. When you get there, look for Jehu son of Jehoshaphat, the son of Nimshi. Go to him, get him away from his companions and take him into an inner room. Then take the flask and pour the oil on his head and declare, 'This is what the LORD says: I anoint you king over Israel.' Then open the door and run; don't delay!"

The messenger having done his job, "Then he opened the door and fled" (v. 10). Seems pretty clear what kind of guy Jehu was! Not the kind of guy you want to give a charge to. And the result was excessive zeal: The problems get worse, so that when

Jehu does react, he is over the top. Hosea addresses it in Hosea 1:4: "Then the Lord said to Hosea, 'Call him Jezreel, because I will soon punish the house of Jehu for the massacre at Jezreel, and I will put an end to the kingdom of Israel.'" He had responded far too aggressively. It is what happens when leadership is too slow to react to a problem, and the mole hill becomes a mountain.

Never got around to it. Like the apostles in Acts 1. Having been given the broad instruction and game plan by Jesus and the angels, they still made no plans despite the last words and repeated commands of Jesus while on earth that they were to go to the ends of the world with the gospel message.

Are we getting and keeping Jesus' vision for his church and his disciples? The text says, "all that Jesus began to do and teach." When he began, the message was clear: Repent, for the kingdom is at hand. "All that Jesus began to do and teach, until the day when he was taken up, after he had given commands through the Holy Spirit to the apostles whom he had chosen" (vv. 1–2 ESV). What were his last commands, his last instructions?

The Greek word is ἐντέλλω *entellō* which means "to enjoin, charge, command, give orders." "Commands" is translated as "instructions" in the NIV, but "commands" or "charges" fits the context better than "instructions."

In all four Gospels, what was Jesus' command after his resurrection and before his ascension?

"Therefore go and make disciples of all nations." (Matthew 28:19)

He said to them, "Go into all the world and preach the gospel to all creation." (Mark 16:15)

Repentance for the forgiveness of sins will be preached in his name to all nations, beginning at Jerusalem. (Luke 24:47)

"As the Father has sent me, I am sending you." And with that he breathed on them and said, "Receive the

Holy Spirit." (John 20:21–22)

Jesus said, "beginning at Jerusalem." Not starting and ending in Jerusalem, but to all nations. That was not so clear to them. His final commands are mission focused! And the place to exercise that mission was to the ends of the earth.

They must have heard what he said but didn't quite understand it. There was a very common expectation that the nations would pour into Jerusalem at the end times. So the apostles' mindset was to stay and get ready for that event. But the New Age now overlaps the Old Age. In this overlap time, we are to go and make disciples of all nations so that (some) people from all the nations will be able to assemble at the New Jerusalem at the end of times. The apostles heard what Jesus said but did not really think he meant for them to go to all nations. Why? I am sure for the same reasons we don't hear it for our lives. Well, I have to raise my children, then, well, I have to stay for my grandchildren or aging parents. We'll get around to it. Let's just have some great programs for the kids and maybe erect a building, and then people will come to us.

It was their role as spiritual leaders to lead everyone out on that mission. It required haste, diligence, and a decisiveness that hears God's commands and leads those following Jesus into obedient action. We cannot be frozen into inaction by criticisms that come our way. In the face of such events and times, spiritual leadership still must act deliberately and diligently and in haste to continue our purpose as leaders in the church.

Spiritual leaders teach what Jesus taught and diligently and zealously obey his final instructions.

What are some applications?

First, we must listen and be aware of what the needs of the people are and pray for discernment. But what seems to be a common practice is to take surveys to ask the people what they want. As Aaron says to a very indignant Moses when he returned with the Ten Commandments, "I just gave the people what they wanted. They wanted to go back to Egypt, so I made them this golden calf" (or as he pathetically said, "I threw the gold into the fire and this golden calf popped out"). Paul predicted that there would come a time when people will not want sound teaching, but will seek those who tell them what they want to hear, having itching ears that they want their leaders to scratch.

Second, spiritual leadership is constantly engaged in moving the people forward. So new plans are needed. Yet at the same time, the leader is sensitive to input from those they lead. In our zeal, we can be ambitious regarding new programs but fail to see the need for moderation or adjustment.

Third, in our zeal and diligence, we are also working on creating an atmosphere of faith, love, and encouragement. We must be careful to be patient and gentle with those who might disagree (2 Timothy 2:25).

Leading with advisers is very different from leading as a committee. With God's help and the mentoring of others, let us move God's people forward.

· Chapter Five ·

Risk-Taking Leadership

"Again, it will be like a man going on a journey, who called his servants and entrusted his wealth to them. To one he gave five bags of gold, to another two bags, and to another one bag, each according to his ability. Then he went on his journey. The man who had received five bags of gold went at once and put his money to work and gained five bags more. So also, the one with two bags of gold gained two more. But the man who had received one bag went off, dug a hole in the ground and hid his master's money.

"After a long time the master of those servants returned and settled accounts with them. The man who had received five bags of gold brought the other five. 'Master,' he said, 'you entrusted me with five bags of gold. See, I have gained five more.'

"His master replied, 'Well done, good and faithful servant! You have been faithful with a few things; I will put you in charge of many things. Come and share your master's happiness!'

"The man with two bags of gold also came. 'Master,' he said, 'you entrusted me with two bags of gold; see, I have gained two more.'

"His master replied, 'Well done, good and faithful servant! You have been faithful with a few things; I will put you in charge of many things. Come and share your master's happiness!'

"Then the man who had received one bag of gold came. 'Master,' he said, 'I knew that you are a hard man, harvesting where you have not sown and gathering where you have not scattered seed. So I was afraid and went out and hid your gold in the ground. See, here is what belongs to you.'

"His master replied, 'You wicked, lazy servant! So you knew that I harvest where I have not sown and gather where I have not scattered seed? Well then, you should have put my money on deposit with the bankers, so that when I returned I would have received it back with interest.

"'So take the bag of gold from him and give it to the one who has ten bags. For whoever has will be given more, and they will have an abundance. Whoever does not have, even what they have will be taken from them. And throw that worthless servant outside, into the darkness, where there will be weeping and gnashing of teeth." (Matthew 25:14–30)

When churches go through turbulent times, and all churches do eventually, there usually is an atmosphere of reluctance and over-cautiousness, trying not to make any mistakes because most are tender and recovering from the upheaval. There are reasons for the fear, but there is not a reason for the lack of faith. And such times may be times of opportunity to advance God's kingdom. The early disciples in Acts 1 were reeling from the events that had happened. Their leader had been crucified. The apostles had all behaved poorly, running for cover and hiding. It is just barely over a month since the terrible scene of the arrest, trial, and crucifixion of Jesus. Yet it will be the very time of some of the most glorious events of the New Testament church, including a spectacular conversion scene with three thousand baptized after one sermon!

Even medically and athletically, how to recover from surgery or a strenuous workout has completely changed. One doesn't just lie there in a hospital bed letting the body heal. There is a new procedure. ERAS, Enhanced Recovery After Surgery, now involves patients getting back on their feet more quickly, which reduces hospital stays and surgical complications. If you have a knee replacement, you do not just lie there and recover slowly, but are forced to get up shortly after the surgery.

There is a natural reluctance to do this because of a concern over the risk of damage. Let someone recover first before you get them on their feet again. Well, not so much in medicine.

Here in the well-known parable of Jesus, the master is going away on a journey. He entrusts to three servants bags of gold (talents): five, two, and one. The distribution is based on the master's perception of their ability. Nothing is expected that is beyond their ability to do. The first servant goes out immediately and invests. No time delay is implied. He doesn't think that since the master is away, he has time to set things up. No, he acts at once and makes a hundred percent profit. The second servant, with his two bags of gold, does the same. In the Gospel of Luke, the profits are even greater. There, each is given one mina, and the first takes that and makes ten, a ten times return. The second makes five times the amount given. The third, however, digs a hole and buries his master's money. He does nothing.

Even in Jesus' day, doubling one's investment in a relatively short time span means that investments were made that involved taking risks. In other words, they were to invest in something that could bring a great return or at the same time, they might lose it all. Making ten times as much would naturally involve even more risk.

The master returns, and the first two servants approach him. The master is understandably pleased. They are called good and faithful servants. Again, faithful: They went out in faith and multiplied what was given.

The third servant, who went and buried the money, claims he did the safe thing. Does doing the "safe" thing please the master? "Safe" and "safe places" is the language of our day. We commend playing it safe. As if following Jesus is ever safe! When did he ever say that? Yes, safe eternally, but not safe living on this planet as his disciple. Jesus forecasts quite the opposite.

In contrast to being a "good and faithful servant," the last servant is described as wicked, lazy and worthless. He has done nothing and blamed his actions on the master, whom he describes as a hard man. Even if he had done the minimum risk taking, putting the money in a bank, at least he would have gotten some interest.

This is a very challenging parable about our responsibility as leaders. What are we doing with what has been entrusted to us? As Paul tells Timothy (2 Timothy 2:2), what you have been entrusted with is meant to be handed down to faithful disciples who will do, teach, and entrust to the next level.

What do we do in tough times? Do we lay low and become overly cautious, afraid to take a risk in studying the Bible, hesitating to call people to a decision because we are so afraid they might not make it? And what are you afraid of? Is it that the master is too hard, or that our people will judge us harshly? Are we good and faithful servants?

There was a time when our churches went through a hard phase of reevaluation and criticism. It wasn't going to be the last time. I was leading a church in Hampton Roads, Virginia. When I saw so many other churches hunkering down and playing it safe, we decided to plant a church that very year. We decided not to give less to world missions, but to give more. It was a very difficult time, but it was also a time, as always, of opportunity. The world was still lost. Our mission was still the same. We didn't lose members in that church that year; our church grew even with a church planting being sent out.

What do we do when our people face spiritual trauma? One thing, for sure, is not to take a break from being with God's people. I don't think I have ever seen that work positively for a Christian's life. It is not an accurate biblical statement to say, "I am not taking a break from God, just his people"! What Bible are you reading?

Another thing is not to stop reading your Bible. Read Acts or 1 Corinthians if you think this is the first time the church has had problems. God forbid you stop giving and spiritualize it as you keep your money and think you are doing the right thing. Giving is giving to God. Jesus commends the widow giving to the temple, funds that employed the very people who would organize Jesus' arrest and death days later. She was simply giving to God.

The time to really make money is not investing in the market when the market is flourishing, but to invest when the market hits its lows. As long as you are in it for the long term, you'll usually be fine. Well, we are following Jesus for the longest of terms—eternity.

In faith and in a faithful way, present the gospel to people and take the risk of calling them to a decision. There is no perfect presentation of the gospel that will make sure that person never leaves the Lord. Most leaders' main problem is no longer retention, but conversions. And the kind of discipling people receive and the examples that they see are just as important a factor for their stability in what happens after their conversion.

Make sure you keep the standards high. Larry W. Hurtado's book *Destroyer of the Gods* discusses why only two religions remained intact after the destruction of the Roman Empire: Judaism and Christianity. He discusses that, to the Romans, the most repulsive part of the Christian message was its exclusiveness. Judaism was also exclusive but received less persecution because the Jews were also seen as a racial subgroup in the empire. But the Christian message was transethnic, touching all parts of the empire. The word "Idolatry," from *eidolon*, "image" or "phantom" (false and deceptive entities unworthy of worship), was a pejorative term to the ears of those who heard the preaching of turning from idolatry to follow the true God. Following Jesus was not just another choice in the pantheon of the gods, it was the only choice. That may be the single most important reason the Romans tried to crush it. As Pliny wrote, it wasn't their teaching but their stubbornness that made him react.

It is very risky having a narrow way and a narrow gate. It invites criticism and persecution. Yet it was the message that the early disciples proclaimed despite the reaction. It is crucial not to try to remove the risk of our message thinking to avoid persecution and gain acceptance. It has the reverse effect. Our ministries will not grow by being more inclusive. They will grow when we proclaim that there is no other way to be saved except by what Jesus did on the cross and we stay true to the biblical teaching concerning connecting to that salvific process. Many sociological scholars have studied this. We need to make sure that we are not ashamed of Jesus, but as Jesus said, not ashamed of his words either. We need to boldly and unapologetically preach Jesus and his words! Not just the red-letter ones, since his words inspired by the Holy Spirit include all the Scriptures.

If our ministries are flat or slowly shrinking, it is time to evaluate our faith and expectation. It is not time to navel gaze but to move forward. The risk, as Jesus points out, is well worth the effort. "Lazy," "wicked," and "worthless" are words that we would hate to hear when the master returns expecting some outcome of our lives. A greeting of, "Welcome, good and faithful servant, please come and rejoice with me," that is what we want to hear.

Are we taking risks? I remember as a young preacher hearing an older minister named Roy Osborne give a sermon in which he shared an experience he had when he took a university course. I don't remember the exact subject, but the professor made the comment, "Surely, no one still believes in the tired old teaching of the Bible and its ethics." There was a quiet, stunned moment, until Roy spoke up and said, "Well there's one who still believes!" After class, several gathered around him and shared that they had the same convictions. Well, why didn't they speak up?

It is time for risk and boldness now as it has always been.

· Chapter Six ·

Staying on Point

When word came to Sanballat, Tobiah, Geshem the Arab and the rest of our enemies that I had rebuilt the wall and not a gap was left in it—though up to that time I had not set the doors in the gates— Sanballat and Geshem sent me this message: "Come, let us meet together in one of the villages on the plain of Ono."

But they were scheming to harm me; so I sent messengers to them with this reply: "I am carrying on a great project and cannot go down. Why should the work stop while I leave it and go down to you?" Four times they sent me the same message, and each time I gave them the same answer.

Then, the fifth time, Sanballat sent his aide to me with the same message, and in his hand was an unsealed letter in which was written:

"It is reported among the nations—and Geshem says it is true—that you and the Jews are plotting to revolt, and therefore you are building the wall. Moreover, according to these reports you are about to become their king and have even appointed prophets to make this proclamation about you in Jerusalem: 'There is a king in Judah!' Now this report will get back to the king; so come, let us meet together."

I sent him this reply: "Nothing like what you are saying is happening; you are just making it up out of your head."

They were all trying to frighten us, thinking, "Their hands will get too weak for the work, and it will not be completed."

But I prayed, "Now strengthen my hands." (Nehemiah 6:1–9)

Then Peter, filled with the Holy Spirit, said to them:.... "Salvation is found in no one else, for there is no other name under heaven given to mankind by which we must be saved."

When they saw the courage of Peter and John and realized that they were unschooled, ordinary men, they were astonished and they took note that these men had been with Jesus. But since they could see the man who had been healed standing there with them, there was nothing they could say. So they ordered them to withdraw from the Sanhedrin and then conferred together. "What are we going to do with these men?" they asked. "Everyone living in Jerusalem knows they have performed a notable sign, and we cannot deny it. But to stop this thing from spreading any further among the people, we must warn them to speak no longer to anyone in this name."

Then they called them in again and commanded them not to speak or teach at all in the name of Jesus. But Peter and John replied, "Which is right in God's eyes: to listen to you, or to him? You be the judges! As for us, we cannot help speaking about what we have seen and heard." (Acts 4:8, 12–20)

There is an innocent notion that when we decide to follow God, everything will go rosy and smooth. Even at our conversion we naively assume that everyone will rejoice over our change. Our parents and old friends will be so impressed with our decision that they will not only be supportive, but some will even begin the process of making that same decision as well. That indeed may happen in a limited sense. But there is also the likelihood that we will be shocked by some of the reactions of family and the pulling away of some friends. Peter was well aware of this possibility: "They are surprised that you do not join them in their reckless, wild living, and they heap abuse on you" (1 Peter 4:4).

From the early church days in Acts 3 and 4 where an undeniable miracle happened in the healing of a well-recognized beggar at the Beautiful Gate, though there was wonder and amazement, this was followed by stern warnings from the authorities. They were determined to stop the spread of the message and truth about Jesus.

One of the functions of spiritual leadership is that, in the face of opposition and problems both within and outside the church, godly leadership will keep everyone on point. And what is the point? As Peter says, nothing will keep us from our main point of proclaiming the good news of Jesus crucified and resurrected for our justification.

I am sure the Jewish leaders did not concern themselves with the benevolent work the church was showing to its members, i.e., the visitors who were converted at Pentecost and the care of the needy such as the widows among them. They didn't tell them to stop meeting at Solomon's Portico in public gatherings. Just stop speaking about Jesus! And not just speaking about him in general, but particularly that he is the only answer, that he is the prophesied Messiah, that there is no other name by which a person can be saved. And nothing should get us off that point. Nothing should make us back away from the exclusive claims of Jesus' lordship, the need for conversion, and what it means to be a disciple.

But distractions do come up. Very early issues of fairness and justice disturbed the church in Acts 6. The early church was not a homogeneous group, despite the fact that they were all Jews at this point. The two groups identified were the Hellenistic and the Hebraic Jews.

In those days when the number of disciples was increasing, the Hellenistic Jews among them complained

> against the Hebraic Jews because their widows were
> being overlooked in the daily distribution of food. So
> the Twelve gathered all the disciples together and said,
> "It would not be right for us to neglect the ministry of
> the word of God in order to wait on tables." (Acts 6:1–2).

Those Jewish (Hebraic) Christian widows who were local were perceived to be getting favorable treatment over the Jewish (Hellenistic) Christian widows who were not local but had been raised in a Greek culture. The context makes it clear that the church was being very successful in the salvation of souls, and their conversions were increasing. The apostles were being distracted and pulled off point by this internal need. Peter in absolutist terms makes it clear that it would not be right for their ministry of the word of God to be disrupted by this issue of justice. They were not going to ignore the problem. They would delegate it to the six men selected to take care of it. They assigned them the task, and judging by their Greek names, gave those in the camp of the grumbling the authority to sort out the problem. But the apostles, the leaders, were not going to get off point.

There is never a time when both inside and outside the church concerns of justice and fairness cease to come up. One of the metaphors for the church is the family of God, and anyone in a family knows that problems of fairness and justice are regular occurrences. In the Roman world of the first century, there were many issues of injustice from slavery, infanticide, Roman privilege, overtaxation, family dysfunction, and others. Yet the mission of the church was to save souls, and what would follow over the years would be the correction of many of those injustices. That is a fact, though some of the points of justice would take many years to correct.

The pull to get off point has occurred all my Christian life. In my early discipleship, there were social justice issues—civil rights and the Vietnam War. On both issues I had a clear position. Yet it was in this atmosphere that our movement started as the real solution to those ills. It is no coincidence that the kickoff moment for our movement was a campus evangelism seminar meeting in Dallas in 1968 called (ambitiously) the International Campus Evangelism Seminar. (Interesting that one year later would be Woodstock, also challenging the values of their parents.) It was a meeting charging campus ministries to get back on point. The state universities were not something to be guarded against, but an opportunity to make disciples to change the world.

There would be other distractions and pulls to get off point. There would be constant leadership issues, pulls to focus inwardly rather than outwardly, dysfunctional leadership, persecution enhanced by the internet, and many others. There would be new issues around the women's role, modern forms of infanticide, and social justice for minorities. What still needs to be our response?

Nehemiah gives us an example of staying on point. He has come to Jerusalem having heard that despite the return of Ezra eleven years earlier, the revival movement that Ezra instigated had bogged down. Nehemiah hears from his brother of the condition and spirit of the returned exiles and the lack of morale in the city of Jerusalem. He gets permission from King Artaxerxes to take a leave of absence and go to Jerusalem for the purpose of rebuilding the wall around the city.

Despite his high position, there arose immediate opposition due to Nehemiah's decision to only allow those seriously following God's word to be involved. The ridicule and opposition started. Nehemiah answered them by saying, "The God of heaven will give us success. We his servants will start rebuilding, but as for you, you have no share in Jerusalem or any claim or historic right to it." (Nehemiah 2:20). In other words, this was going to be a narrow way with a narrow gate.

Eventually, after failed attempts to intimidate and a letter written with false charges, the opposition approached Nehemiah to work together. There wasn't really any serious attempt at unity, nor would Nehemiah have any part of it. The invitation was offered to come and meet together on the plain of Ono (at a crucial moment with the walls having been rebuilt and all that remained were the gates to be built).

"Oh no to the plain of Ono" is Nehemiah's response. "I am doing a good work, why should I stop to talk to you?" Five times this occurs!

Spiritual leadership holds on to the trustworthy sayings floating around the New Testament church: "Here is a trustworthy saying that deserves full acceptance: Christ Jesus came into the world to save sinners—of whom I am the worst" (1 Timothy 1:15).

Full acceptance means letting nothing move us off our mission, and full acceptance of this is required; in other words, everyone needs to get on board.

Let's look at some practical points.

Of course we are always working at being fair. God ordains the governments of the world to work for justice, and Christians support justice. But our message is not about justice per se, since by God's standard of justice, we all fall far short of the glory of God. There is no one righteous. So let us continue to preach the grace of God.

It is important to be good listeners, but it is also our purpose when we hear the distractions that affect disciple's lives (and there are many), to redirect them to keep their eyes on Jesus who came to seek and save the lost.

Culture always influences followers of Christ. But having recognized that, we also remind ourselves that we are out to change culture, not be led by it. We need to be raising the issue that really counts in people's lives and that is of far most importance: their relationship with God. Jesus asked 307 questions of his listeners. He was asked 183 and only answered three. As one of my professors (Dr. Geoffrey Bromley) once remarked, the problem with apologetics is that we let the world ask the questions rather than us taking the initiative and asking the *right* questions. Let's ask questions about the eternal issues, the questions that matter most. These questions in a thousand years for an individual will be the ones that still concern them. All the other issues will be done and dusted.

In Acts 4 Peter and John are instructed not to speak any more in his name, and their response is that in the sight of God (not these religious leaders' sight), they cannot be silent. After more threats, they returned to their friends, who undoubtedly would have been very concerned. They prayed, and the room shook (Acts 4:31). The shakeup began after they demonstrated faith, not before, just like the action of Jonathan and his armor bearer, whose steps of faith in attacking the Philistines at Micmash was followed by an earthquake.

I believe God always wants to shake things up. But faith precedes God's response. It is time to faithfully step out in our mission to the lost. What follows will be God's applause!

· Chapter Seven ·

Doing the Work of an Evangelist

But you, keep your head in all situations, endure hardship, do the work of an evangelist, discharge all the duties of your ministry. (2 Timothy 4:5)

Although this is addressed to Timothy as he serves as an evangelist, it teaches us principles that apply to all spiritual leadership.

The first work of spiritual leadership is keeping your head in all situations. The poem voted most popular in the UK in a poll by the BBC was overwhelmingly Rudyard Kipling's poem "IF."

If you can keep your head when all about you
Are losing theirs and blaming it on you,
If you can trust yourself when all men doubt you,
But make allowance for their doubting too;
If you can wait and not be tired by waiting,
Or being lied about, don't deal in lies,
Or being hated don't give way to hating,
And yet don't look too good, nor talk too wise;

If you can dream—and not make dreams your master;
If you can think—and not make thoughts your aim;
If you can meet with Triumph and Disaster
And treat those two impostors just the same;
If you can bear to hear the truth you've spoken

Twisted by knaves to make a trap for fools,
Or watch the things you gave your life to, broken,
And stoop and build 'em up with worn-out tools.

Keeping our head in all situations always stands out about leadership, even in the eyes of the world. Ernest Shackleton's leadership of his stranded crew in the Antarctic when his ship was icebound was a great example of keeping your head in all situations. He kept his crew alive over two years until rescued, from 1914 to 1916, not losing one man.

As a disciple one does not, of course, trust oneself as Kipling writes. Our trust is not in man but in God. But the principles in general do apply for us. Spiritual leaders do not panic. They do not hide in the nooks and crannies when Goliath-sized problems arise.

What is our work as leaders?

First, one must keep their priorities straight. Over the years the word "priority" has changed its meaning and has been redefined. In his best-selling book, *Essentialism*, Greg McKeown explains the surprising history of the word and how its meaning has shifted over time.

> The word "priority" came into the English language in the 1400s. It was singular. It meant the very first or prior thing. It stayed singular for the next five hundred years. Only in the 1900s did we pluralize the term and start talking about priorities. Illogically, we reasoned that by changing the word we could bend reality. Somehow we would now be able to have multiple "first" things.

This has obviously slipped into our church language. We talk about our priorities, rightly putting God first, but not understanding that all other pursuits and interests are not another priority, and while being important, are not on the same level as seeking God. You cannot "balance" seeking first the kingdom with anything else. There is no balance, yet the language slips into our vocabulary as part of "healthy spiritual language." Balance and boundaries (important concepts) are not on the other side of the scale of seeking first the kingdom.

As Paul describes the work of spiritual leaders in several metaphors in 2 Timothy 2, one is the soldier: "No one serving as a soldier gets entangled in civilian affairs, but rather tries to please his commanding officer" (v. 4). He is not doing the ministry plus doing something else. He is not doing two jobs at the same time unless the situation requires it due to lack of funds, an example Paul gave. He worked at tentmaking until funds came from Philippi, then he worked full time in Corinth. He did not do both once the funds were there. Not to get entangled in the world is a challenge Jesus gave to all of us, pursuing treasure on earth rather than treasure in heaven. Again, what is our priority is the issue.

Second, spiritual leadership is Word centered. "I charge you in the presence of God and of Christ Jesus, who is to judge the living and the dead, and by his appearing and his kingdom: preach the word; be ready in season and out of season; reprove, rebuke, and exhort, with complete patience and teaching" (2 Timothy 4:1 ESV). Spiritual leadership uses the Scriptures all the time, in season and out. We are bound by this ruler, this canon (which is what canon means). Our lessons are not anecdotal chicken soup for the soul's emotional entertainment. We are good listeners, but we use God's word in our interactions and discipling. "Let the word of Christ dwell in you richly, teaching and admonishing one another" (Colossians 3:16a). It is helping others apply to their lives the commands and principles they agreed to follow at their baptism. We say amen when someone says they believe that Jesus rose from the grave. But we shout amen when they make their good confession that Jesus is Lord. Discipling follows, as described in Matthew 28:18-20, as after baptism we teach people to obey what they have accepted. The mind has agreed; the heart and will need to follow. We teach and admonish, "admonish" being the Greek word *noutheteo,* "to place on the mind." Teaching is imparting information, while admonishment is for heart change. Paul is totally convinced; he says in Romans 15:14,

"I myself am satisfied about you, my brothers, that you yourselves are full of goodness, filled with all knowledge and able to instruct (*noutheteo*) one another." Spiritual leadership involves passing on the message to reliable, faithful Christians, who then can pass that on to others (2 Timothy 2:2). Our task is to raise up other spiritual leaders. Failure to do that is not fulfilling one key task of leadership.

Third, our work in spiritual leadership is to lead in such a way that the gospel gets to the marketplace. Mark 6:56–7:1 says of Jesus, "And wherever he came, in villages, cities, or countryside, they laid the sick in the marketplaces and implored him that they might touch even the fringe of his garment. And as many as touched it were made well.... The Pharisees gathered to him (to criticize him)."

Marketplaces are where both the religious and nonreligious have to go to survive and where they slightly interact. We must get food at a common spot. The marketplace is where Jesus healed the sick, the very place you would not want the sick to be, next to all the food you wanted to buy (no masks in those days). The religious people, here the Pharisees, had the view that you went to the market, but went in and got out as quickly as possible to keep a distance lest you get contaminated.

In the late sixties and early seventies, state universities were treated by religious people as places where you had to go if you couldn't afford private education at a Christian college. But the safest thing to do was to go in and go out as quickly as possible (and if you really cared about your kids, you would send them to a Christian school). Christian student centers were built so that those not fortunate enough to go a Christian university might have a safe place to go and not be contaminated by the secular and godless universities that were out to destroy their faith and morality. Academic classes would be taught there on site, called Bible Chairs. It was their version of what we call creating "safe places." But at some point in the sixties, many followers of Christ decided to change their perspective. Let's not just build a Christian student center for protection, let's go to the marketplace to do our ministry. What was the marketplace? Dorms and student unions. So Bible studies were begun in the dorms, late at night where the people who needed God were. Meetings were held in the student union, a place every student visited regularly. It brought about a revival among the young people who were on those campuses that affected the whole church (sometimes positively and sometimes negatively). But that is the job of spiritual leadership. It must train and teach other disciples to be in the world but not of the world. It must not just train them to survive the world, but equip them to change it. As Proverbs 28:1 states, "The wicked flee though no one pursues, but the righteous are as bold as a lion." Rather than fleeing, leadership commits to bringing the gospel to those same marketplaces and being as bold as lions—disciples who are not of the world but are in the world, impacting it for God and bringing the good news of salvation and healing for the troubled and confused.

Even when what we build is torn down, we seek to rebuild. That is the biblical view of God's work throughout the Old Testament and church history. And our campus ministries and those working in the marketplace need to be empowered to again cease to be "safe" and to go into harm's way, like a Desmond Doss, a medic in WWII, who continually went into harm's way just to save one more soul.

· Chapter Eight ·

Dealing with Conflict

Leadership will inevitably lead to some conflict. Dealing with conflict in the ministry in a spiritual way is just as critical as learning how to deal with conflict in our marriages and families. Not dealing with conflict in a spiritual way will end poorly. Proverbs 19:11 (ESV), "Good sense makes one slow to anger, and it is his glory to overlook an offense," teaches us that there are times to just overlook offenses. In fact, in general, we must learn to overlook slights and offenses that occur in all relationships. But there are critical times when we should not do so. The failure to address conflict lets Satan introduce bitter roots that will only defile the fellowship. Time does not heal all wounds!

If the spring that flows out of our hearts is bitter, we need to bring in the salt of the word of God to bring health and life (2 Kings 2:19–22). And we are all called to be that salt, that instrument that God uses to bring peace.

> When Cephas came to Antioch, I opposed him to his face, because he stood condemned. For before certain men came from James, he used to eat with the Gentiles. But when they arrived, he began to draw back and separate himself from the Gentiles because he was afraid of those who belonged to the circumcision group. The other Jews joined him in his hypocrisy, so that by their hypocrisy even Barnabas was led astray.

When I saw that they were not acting in line with the truth of the gospel, I said to Cephas in front of them all, "You are a Jew, yet you live like a Gentile and not like a Jew. How is it, then, that you force Gentiles to follow Jewish customs?" (Galatians 2:11–14)

Certain people came down from Judea to Antioch and were teaching the believers: "Unless you are circumcised, according to the custom taught by Moses, you cannot be saved." This brought Paul and Barnabas into sharp dispute and debate with them. So Paul and Barnabas were appointed, along with some other believers, to go up to Jerusalem to see the apostles and elders about this question. The church sent them on their way....

Then some of the believers who belonged to the party of the Pharisees stood up and said, "The Gentiles must be circumcised and required to keep the law of Moses." The apostles and elders met to consider this question. (Acts 15:1–3, 5–6)

Some time later Paul said to Barnabas, "Let us go back and visit the believers in all the towns where we preached the word of the Lord and see how they are doing." Barnabas wanted to take John, also called Mark, with them, but Paul did not think it wise to take him, because he had deserted them in Pamphylia and had not continued with them in the work. They had such a sharp disagreement that they parted company. Barnabas took Mark and sailed for Cyprus, but Paul chose Silas and left, commended by the believers to the grace of the Lord. (Acts 15:36–40)

Let's consider several points about spiritual conflict.

First, it is important to differentiate between conflict over real issues and conflict over personalities.

There has been a tendency to assume that the real issue in

conflict is always about personalities. If you can reconcile the personal conflict, the supposed issue will disappear. It is a fact that there can be personality clashes. The last scripture listed involved a conflict between Paul and Barnabas. There wasn't a theological issue. It was very practically based. Mark had accompanied Barnabas and Paul on their first missionary journey. He got homesick (or something) very early and returned to Jerusalem. We know that John Mark was from a wealthy family. He lived in a gated house with servants. After going through Cyprus, Mark, according to Paul, "deserted" them—a strongly negative Greek word, ἀποστασία *apostasía* ("apostasy"). John Mark was Barnabas's cousin. Barnabas, known for his encouraging nature, wanted to give Mark a second chance. He had done the same thing with Paul himself, when no one would trust that Saul the persecutor had really been converted (Acts 9:27). Paul and Barnabas had a sharp disagreement. They definitely had different personalities! The result was a separation, though not a permanent break. In fact, Paul would write in his last epistle to have Mark come and visit him in prison, describing him as someone useful. I am sure in the sharp dispute Paul was very blunt with Barnabas about what he thought of Mark's behavior and character. Most likely Barnabas defended Mark and argued for giving him a second chance. We all need second chances, not only in regard to our salvation but in any area we seek to change in our character. But I also surmise that after they split, when Barnabas was alone with John Mark, he had a few things to say about his character. And the discipling process worked!

But in the beginning of this same chapter, there were some real theological issues. Does someone have to be circumcised as well as being baptized? Is it mandatory? This was no small issue, but was at the very heart of the gospel. Are we saved by faith or saved by the Law? Must one become a Jew as well as a Christian?

There are times when there just isn't any wiggle room. Paul was well aware of this when Peter was visiting the Galatian churches. The visit was going well, as one might assume, having the "Rock" visit one's church. All went well until certain men came from James, the leader of the Jerusalem church, with a great concern not to have their Jewish mission field made more difficult by what could be stumbling blocks to those they were reaching out to in Jerusalem. It was a real concern; however, sound doctrine and the "necessary inference" practices from that doctrine could not be compromised even for the sake of outreach. So in a very direct way; in fact, so direct most of us would have cringed, Paul got in his face (seems literally). There was not going to be some behind-the-scenes gossip and discussion. No, the elephant in the room needed to be addressed. And Paul was going to be the agent for God even to the "Rock."

The same pattern is seen in Acts 15. Paul and Barnabas addressed the doctrinal issue head on. There seems to be a general understanding that such serious issues needed to be addressed head on rather than just hoping things would work out. There is an Australian saying, "Near enough, good enough," that has produced some less-than-best work practices. But this issue needed to be addressed.

> But some men came down from Judea and were teaching the brothers, "Unless you are circumcised according to the custom of Moses, you cannot be saved." And after Paul and Barnabas had no small dissension and debate with them, Paul and Barnabas and some of the others were appointed to go up to Jerusalem to the apostles and the elders about this question. So, being sent on their way by the church... (Acts 15:1–3 ESV)

"No small dissension and debate" must have been quite a discussion. I contend that this is exactly what we occasionally need to have with others when there are serious issues to discuss. And the fear that this might lead to serious division is a fear that actually produces what it fears. There was a period when our churches went through a tumultuous time. I was amazed to see how different types of people handled the turbulence. One general observation was that those who had spoken up honestly about their convictions and had regularly gotten in trouble actually fared better than those who had stuffed their convictions and damaged their consciences. There was less likely an opportunity for bitterness in the first group because they had stood up. But those who had compromised their consciences fled like hired hands. As iron sharpens iron, so we need to forge our unity, and that means some very hot and direct discussions.

There is a spiritual song that has as a chorus line: "Run to the fight and hold each other tight!" That reflects the instruction that Jesus gave for conflict resolution. If someone has something against you, leave your gift at the altar and run to the fight (Matthew 5:23–24). If you have serious concerns about someone's life, run to the fight and go have a talk (Matthew 18:15). In other words, we are to engage, not run away!

Matthew 18 gives us some specific instructions:

> "If your brother sins against you, go and tell him his fault, between you and him alone. If he listens to you, you have gained your brother. But if he does not listen, take one or two others along with you, that every charge may be established by the evidence of two or three witnesses. If he refuses to listen to them, tell it to the church. And if he refuses to listen even to the church, let him be to you as a Gentile and a tax collector. Truly, I say to you, whatever you bind on earth shall be bound in heaven, and whatever you loose on earth shall be loosed in heaven." (Matthew 18:15–18 ESV)

So, here are some practicals.

Pray for guidance about when to engage. If it is good to overlook an offense, then determine if what is bothering you should be overlooked. But if it continues to affect you and your conscience, then it is time to talk. Better to talk than to let some things simmer. They will boil over. As "watchmen," there is a responsibility to sound the alarm (Ezekiel 33).

Continue to build an accepted practice that if someone wants to talk to you, you need to talk. Don't play the pseudo-psychology line and refuse to have the discussion by saying you don't feel safe. Again, following Jesus is not safe as the world defines safe.

But that doesn't mean you have to sit there and be abused. There is meant to be dialogue, but humble dialogue aimed at figuring out what someone is trying to say to you about your character. It is fine to respond, but only after you have really listened intently.

Don't be frozen into inaction by fears of what might happen. If you are doing the right thing, then the matter will be settled. If the worst happens, it happens. But the most important thing is to be true to God and his word. Once in India there were problems from disgruntled members. Others were encouraged to address the problems with them, but they expressed the fear of them reacting and leaving. Whether they left or not was not the issue. God's word and its direction for us was the issue. There are times when we must be true to God's word no matter what the cost. When Jesus was told that what he was saying was offensive to those in John 6 who had sought him out, his response was, "If that offends you, try this!" Jesus had no reluctance to shrink down his group of followers. He knew that if the standards stay high, the masses will come.

Don't be afraid to get others involved. There are times to bring a witness, and there are times to even present the issue to the church. Others involved can help to clarify the issues and reduce what feels personal.

Understand that Jesus expects us to resolve differences even if those we differ with are on the other side of the world. In the Matthew passage, what is bound on earth biblically is bound in heaven. You are in a local congregation (hopefully) but still part of the church universal. The Matthew passage addresses the church universal by the language used. There, in fact, was no local church when Jesus taught these conflict resolution practicals.

Again, problems are meant to be addressed, not ignored. Ignoring them in the long run is a more serious problem than over-addressing them. Jesus told a parable about a widow pleading for justice from a godless judge. Her persistent pleading brought her justice. If he eventually gives justice, how much more, Jesus said, would God bring justice. And not just bring it, but bring it speedily.

And the Lord said, "Hear what the unrighteous judge says. And will not God give justice to his elect, who cry to him day and night? Will he delay long over them? I tell you, he will give justice to them speedily. Nevertheless, when the Son of Man comes, will he find faith on earth?" (Luke 18:6–8 ESV)

Address conflict "speedily." Too often we fearfully let unresolved conflicts linger. We think it will all work out, but it is a case of:

"They have healed the wound of my people lightly,
saying, 'Peace, peace,'
when there is no peace." (Jeremiah 6:14)

When I was growing up, most skinned knee remedies were painful. I used to seek some relief from my parents. Just blow on it was my remedy. Of course, their remedy involved a medicine that stung! Conflict resolution can be a painful process, but far less painful than an infectious attitude or practice that can cause permanent soul damage.

Conflicts came and will continue to regularly occur. Spiritual leadership deals with them so that the church stays fully united in mind and judgment.

· Chapter Nine ·

Integrity: Guarding Your Heart

Integrity: the state of being whole and undivided; Latin *integer*, "whole." When it comes to our character, it means that what we are on the outside is the same as what we are on the inside.

We know that God shows his integrity in all that he does.

> The Rock, his work is perfect,
> for all his ways are justice.
> A God of faithfulness and without iniquity,
> just and upright is he. (Deuteronomy 32:4 ESV)

> For the word of the LORD is upright,
> and all his work is done in faithfulness. (Psalm 33:4 ESV)

God is always the same in all parts of his nature.

We can see it in his creation. You can tell a banana by its skin. When you peel it, you are going to find the same thing every time. But what is true of fruit is not true of people. From the beginning of biblical times, we learn of God's intention: "So God created mankind in his own image, in the image of God he created him; male and female he created them" (Genesis 1:27).

So man and woman were made to have the same integrity that God has both on the outside and inside. Most are familiar with what follows. They are tempted to eat the forbidden fruit.

"For God knows that when you eat from it your eyes will be opened, and you will be like God, knowing good and evil."

When the woman saw that the fruit of the tree was good for food and pleasing to the eye, and also desirable for gaining wisdom, she took some and ate it. She also gave some to her husband, who was with her, and he ate it. Then the eyes of both of them were opened, and they realized they were naked; so they sewed fig leaves together and made coverings for themselves. (Genesis 3:5–7)

So we have the first split in the integrity we were meant to have, that God planned. There is a literal first cover-up. There is a divide now between the outer and inner person that affects both sexes.

In Greek theater, acting was done more like we do animation films. The actors wore masks to reflect their moods. There was a Greek theater in Sepphoris, which was a regional Roman-Greek administrative center about five kilometers (a little over three miles) from Nazareth. The most recent evaluations have Sepphoris with a population of between 2000 and 4300, and Nazareth with a population of approximately 480. Since Nazareth was just a small village, one can only assume that Joseph, Jesus, and the other brothers worked as carpenters in Sepphoris on regular occasions.

The word "hypocrite" in classical and Hellenistic Greek referred to an actor. "ὑποκριτής *hypokritês* [hypocrite], *hypokritês* means "actor," probably as one who interprets a poet, depicting by his whole conduct the role assigned (TDNT).

It was not used in the Old Testament. In the Septuagint, the early Greek translation of the Old Testament, it was used twice. "Everyone utters lies to his neighbor; with flattering lips and *a double heart* they speak" (Psalm 12:2, emphasis added).

And in the NIV and ESV English translations it is only translated once in the Old Testament in Psalm 26:4: "I do not sit with men of falsehood, nor do I consort with hypocrites."

The Hebrew word translated "hypocrite" is עָלַם *'ālam*, which means "to be hidden, concealed, secret." The only other place where it is used is Psalm 90:8, where one gets the same meaning: "You have set our iniquities before you, our *secret sins* in the light of your presence" (emphasis added).

It is Jesus who brings the Greek word "hypocrite" (actor) as a spiritual term for one who is acting out their religion. They put on the mask of religion, but inside they are completely different.

> In the meantime, when so many thousands of the people had gathered together that they were trampling one another, he began to say to his disciples first, "Beware of the leaven of the Pharisees, which is hypocrisy. Nothing is covered up that will not be revealed, or hidden that will not be known." (Luke12:1–2 ESV; see also Matthew 6:2, 7:5, 23:28).

Paul uses it only twice, in Galatians 2:13, "The other Jews joined him in his hypocrisy, so that by their hypocrisy even Barnabas was led astray," and in 1 Timothy 4:2. Peter used it once, perhaps following that convicting moment given by Paul, in 1 Peter 2:1: "So put away all malice and all deceit and hypocrisy and envy and all slander" (ESV).

Living the double life has plagued religious people of all brands since Adam and Eve. It affects all Christians, but the temptation especially applies to spiritual leadership: "Do as I say, not as I do"; "Rules for thee and not for me." To lead always presents the possibility of being whitewashed limestone tombs that look great in the sunshine of Israel, yet being at the same time filled with dead men's bones. It's easy to slip into this mode, like Abraham telling Sarai to say she is his sister, like David thinking he can mess up with Bathsheba and no one will be aware, and like Judas serving as an apostle and treasurer, yet all kinds of things must have been going through his heart.

What are some safeguards for spiritual leadership?

First, above all, guard our hearts. "Above all else, guard your heart, for everything you do flows from it" (Proverbs 4:23).

The stress is from the inside out, not the outside in. Religion is concerned with the outside first. Jesus is concerned with the inside first and foremost. The word of God is meant to affect our hearts first before it affects our behavior (Hebrews 4:12). One should not be absolute about this in that we need to be obedient even when our heart is not where it should be. But where we are meant to live is first of all constantly working on our heart, letting God's word be like a mirror to us that will affect how we act (James 1:22-25). Thus we work from the inside out.

Second, in this process of guarding your heart, you must have others around you to give you insight about what you need to be guarding against.

> See to it, brothers and sisters, that none of you has a sinful, unbelieving heart that turns away from the living God. But encourage one another daily, as long as it is called "Today," so that none of you may be hardened by sin's deceitfulness. We have come to share in Christ, if indeed we hold our original conviction firmly to the very end. (Hebrews 3:12-14)

> For we have come to share in Christ, if indeed we hold our original confidence firm to the end. (v. 14 ESV)

The charge is clear for us not only to guard our hearts personally, but as brothers and sisters, to guard each other's hearts as well. Why? Because sin is deceitful, and the most common, prevalent, and deadly sin is self-deceit. Pride is a good example. In Psalm 73:6 Asaph writes: "Therefore pride is their necklace." One wears a necklace, and everyone sees it except the one who is wearing it. Isn't pride exactly like that! Even the world sees it clearly—how much more those who follow Jesus? But it is not just the self-deceit of pride, but also how we treat people, especially our spouses and children and those we lead.

How we relate to the opposite sex is another area to be on guard. Some of the great names in the Scriptures tripped up on that point. Adam, the first man, Samson, the strongest man, David the man with a pure heart, and Solomon, the wisest man, are all examples. We need trusted brothers and sisters (men to men, women to women) and trusted spouses who know our heart and help expose our secrets.

Personal finances are not meant to be some secret area that no one can touch. A psychologist once said that someone could be sharing the most intimate sexual information with him without hesitation. But once he asked one of his patients about their personal finances only to get a quick retort: "That's none of your business!" As has often been said, "The purse strings and heartstrings are connected."

As the writer of Hebrews said in 12:14, this honesty with another disciple or disciples enables us to "hold our original conviction," our "original confidence" firm to the end. Firm? How many times have we all swayed and drifted from our original convictions? Maybe our fellowship's greatest need is to go back to their original convictions about the need for someone to help disciple them to Jesus.

"Sincerity" is the usual translation of the Greek word εἰλικρίνεια heilikríneia [purity]. Formed from *heílē* ("warmth or light of the sun") and *krínō* ("to test"), these words mean "tested by sunlight," i.e., "pure," and "purity" (TDNT).

"Sincerity," according to folk etymology is from the Latin *sine*, "without" and *cere*, "wax." Wax was said to be used to hide the cracks in pottery or art works and then was glazed over. One could see the flaws if the object were held to the light. Thus the pot without wax was sincere, that is, genuine both on the surface and below (there are many variations of the definition).

The Greek word *heilikrineia* has a somewhat similar meaning etymologically. As disciples, we need to have our lives tested by the light of the gospel. The Gospel of John uses this language of testing:

> This is the verdict: Light has come into the world, but people loved darkness instead of light because their deeds were evil. Everyone who does evil hates the light, and will not come into the light for fear that

their deeds will be exposed. But whoever lives by the truth comes into the light, so that it may be seen plainly that what they have done has been done in the sight of God. (John 3:19–21)

Sunlight and Son light are great disinfectants. As Supreme Court Justice Louis Brandeis said over a century ago, "Sunlight is said to be the best of disinfectants." That was about transparency in government, but how much more do we need the light of Jesus shining in our hearts? Transparency should be a mark of spiritual leadership and discipleship.

Paul uses Moses as an illustration of the history of religious folk covering up: "Since we have such a hope, we are very bold. We are not like Moses, who would put a veil over his face to prevent the Israelites from seeing the end of what was passing away" (2 Corinthians 3:12–13).

Moses had come down from the mountain of the Lord, and there was a radiance from his face from being in the presence of God that the Israelites could not bear to see. So Moses placed a veil over his face to allow them to be in his presence. What this verse in Corinthians says is that when the radiance began to diminish, Moses kept the veil on to prevent them seeing the brilliance fade.

That is the history of all of us regarding our spiritual life. It begins with glory, but it fades. We learn to cover up, having learned the language of church and how to behave in church, while the slow hardening of our hearts and the gradual reduction of confession of sin take place. We want people to think we are fine, but in our hearts there is another story.

Being transparent, judged by the light, is not about being perfect. As Paul says in the next chapter, the light has shined in the darkness of our hearts. The gospel is a treasure in our hearts. But we are still jars of clay. And even when there are cracks, that is where the light shines out to the world. In our honesty and humility about our flaws and sins, these end up being tools to further testify about the power of God to change our lives.

So let us be spiritual leaders who, by their integrity and honesty, shine bright for our Lord in all that we say and do.

· Chapter Ten ·

Leading from the Front

> And the LORD will make you the head and not the tail, and you shall only go up and not down, if you obey the commandments of the LORD your God, which I command you today, being careful to do them, and if you do not turn aside from any of the words that I command you today, to the right hand or to the left, to go after other gods to serve them. (Deuteronomy 28:13–14 ESV)

Moses was speaking to the nation of Israel. There is a conditional promise given to God's people that if they are faithful and obedient, they will not follow the nations, but the nations will follow them. This was a commandment they had much difficulty obeying, as they copied their neighbors, rather than the neighboring countries copying them. But what was true for them as God's people is true for us. Are we out front, faithfully leading and obeying his commands? Or is the culture (the nations) dictating and controlling the church's agenda? Are we being the least important part, the tail, rather than being at the head, leading God's people forward? To change the metaphor slightly, are a few grumblers and complainers, the tail, wagging the dog, the church? Are we changing the world or is the world (the nations) changing the church? The prophet Isaiah, prophesying about the condition of Israel, writes:

For the LORD of hosts has a day
> against all that is proud and lofty,
> against all that is lifted up—and it shall be
brought low;...
And the haughtiness of man shall be humbled,
> and the lofty pride of men shall be brought low,
> and the LORD alone will be exalted in that day.
(Isaiah 2:12, 17 ESV)

What applies to the nation of Israel also applies to spiritual leadership.

In a conversation with an elder's wife fifty years ago concerning the topic and importance of leadership, her simple response from her Old Testament study clearly showed a pattern. If the king of Israel was faithful, so followed the people. If the king was not, the people were affected. So before you blame your people, have a good look at your own leadership. Are you leading from the rear or from the front? Are you proactive, reactive, or inactive? Are you hiding in the middle trying to please everyone?

During the early chapters of Isaiah, the condition of Jerusalem (Judah) was sad. Judah had drifted, following the ways of her sister, Israel. The revival of Uzziah that started so gloriously had floundered as Uzziah got older. "But after Uzziah became powerful, his pride led to his downfall. He was unfaithful to the Lord his God" (2 Chronicles 26:16). It is when Uzziah dies that Isaiah sees the Lord (Isaiah 6:1). What follows this manifestation of God to Isaiah is his humble response to God's holiness in v. 5: "And I said: 'Woe is me! For I am lost, for I am a man of unclean lips; and I dwell in the midst of a people of unclean lips; for my eyes have seen the King, the Lord of hosts!'" (ESV).

In the earlier chapters of Isaiah, Uzziah's downfall of pride is seen (Isaiah 2:12, 17). This spiritual decline resulted in a time when no one wanted to lead:

> For a man will take hold of his brother
> in the house of his father, saying:
> "You have a cloak;

> you shall be our leader,
> and this heap of ruins
>   shall be under your rule";
> in that day he will speak out, saying:
>   "I will not be a healer;
> in my house there is neither bread nor cloak;
>   you shall not make me
>   leader of the people."
> For Jerusalem has stumbled,
>   and Judah has fallen,
> because their speech and their deeds
>   are against the LORD,
> defying his glorious presence. (Isaiah 3:6–8 ESV)

In tough times, the temptation is always to hide in the crowd, to hide in the temple rather than stepping up. What follows is that no one wants to be in leadership. If the example is lacking of leading faithfully from the front, God's people will be affected. Fewer will want the full-time ministry. Instead of a queue to be selected for the ministry, there are numerous ministry jobs and no one to fill them. Churches search for men and women to fill their depleted staff positions. Rather than leading from the front to change the world, everyone hides. In their minds, the condition of the people is too hopeless for anyone to do any good. "Let someone else do it, but not me. And by the way, look how those who try to step up are treated."

It is in this environment when no one wants to stand up for God and lead his people that God asks Isaiah the well-known question: "'Whom shall I send? And who will go for us?' And [Isaiah] said, 'Here am I. Send me!'" (Isaiah 6:8).

At a time when no one wants to lead, "I will step forward," says Isaiah. "Here am I!" It is a text often preached, a theme of many a conference. It is the kind of heart that God is looking for as he searches the world for someone to stand in the gap (Ezekiel 22:30). Spiritual leaders step up. Spiritual leadership leads from the front. Someone stands up for God! It is the context of the account of David's mighty men in 2 Samuel 23:8ff. Battle scenes are described. All the Israelites are running, but these men stand their ground alone.

There is a real danger of a leader taking off on his own and expecting the church to mindlessly follow him. Every leader needs both local and outside input to make sure they have not fallen into self-deceit and delusional leadership. But the kind of leader who goes astray is fairly rare. A greater danger, by far, is when God's people have "hired hands" leading, and the committee in its various forms has stifled anyone who tries to lead the flock to greener pastures and quality spiritual life.

So what does it mean to lead from the front, and what is required?

First, it takes many of the qualities already discussed in earlier chapters of this book. One must be a person of courage, faith, and spirituality, someone who is all about God getting the glory and his name being glorified, not about making a name for themself. It requires those who step up to acknowledge that the issue is on us and not on God. It is not a God problem! The harvest is plentiful, but the workers are few. I believe Jesus says this is applicable to every culture on this earth. Therefore, the buck stops with us. Will I volunteer because we are distressed at the state of leadership or the lack of it? Or will I just be a complainer about the condition of God's church and involved in talks about the problems of the church but taking no action toward the solutions? Will I choose to pull everyone forward, rather than the endless task of trying to get everyone ready before we do something? We will never be ready! Do I think the issue is understanding the culture, the next generation, rather than the real issue of concentrating on understanding what God wants me to do and say?

Second, we must look for others who share God's vision for his people. It will never be the majority, but work with those who want to move forward, and by your example and their example, pull those along who don't have the faith. The same tide will lift all vessels, and we can move people forward from the positions where they are stuck. It is not about pushing them forward, but pulling them. My wife and I have often moved to a ministry that was stuck and divided. The example we set changed everyone's expectations of what God can do. Be a spiritual leader that can change a church or region from even your small discussion group. You can make a difference.

Keep in contact with others who are trying to lead from the front both locally and regionally. The very nature of leading from the front can emotionally leave one feeling isolated and alone. It is how Moses, Elijah, and the Apostle Paul felt at times. "I am the only one, oh Lord!" "All have deserted me, oh Lord"! You must decide to break out of that and reach outside your box to find a likeminded leader, not only for your own good but the good of others. Maybe I'm not on the right track because I am emotionally involved in my local situation, and I cannot see as clearly as I should. I need to talk to someone who is leading in a healthy, growing way. The church is filled with disciples who are meant to be in God's kingdom, under his reign. It is not a democratic institution as we understand democratic governments from our cultures. The King and head of the church is Jesus, not the local leader or regional leader. We don't take votes on the commandments of God. We don't change the commands when they are no longer popular. We work toward consensus but are not led by consensus. It is very important to have a broad leadership platform with evangelists, women's ministry leaders, elders, and deacons to help keep us from being self-deceived about our latest plan.

To the physics question of which is easier, pushing or pulling, in general there is no difference. Rear-wheel drive versus front-wheel drive is similar. It is the Ancient Near Eastern shepherding model of the shepherd leading from the front versus the modern model of sheep dogs and other methods of driving the sheep from the rear. The one clear difference is that the sheep choose to follow rather than are driven. So the outcomes for a while might be the same, but not in the long run, as that house of cards eventually collapses (consider Solomon's abuse of power). We need to be such leaders that our people choose to follow rather than submit to being driven. It is a fact that over the long haul, they must choose, since anyone can leave by their own volition.

What enables them to choose wisely is to have the kind of leaders that set the example. Spiritual leaders set an example for the people! We practice what we preach, proving our genuineness. Our eyes are fixed on Jesus, the founder and perfecter of our faith. And we have to be determined to follow him and his reason for becoming man and saving us from our sins.

Several years ago, I visited a country property where sheep were raised across ten thousand acres. The owner took us out in his ute (that's what we call a utility vehicle in Australia), family riding in the back. Everywhere we went, the sheep ran from us. As we approached one fenced paddock, the sheep ran to us, not away from us. I asked why the change in the sheep's behavior. The owner said, "Well, we've been feeding those sheep."

If we feed the sheep as we lead, they run to us. If we don't feed them, well?

Let us lead from the front, guiding the people to green pastures. If we feed and serve, they will follow God!

· Chapter Eleven ·

Leading with Courage

They had Peter and John brought before them and began to question them: "By what power or what name did you do this?"

Then Peter, filled with the Holy Spirit, said to them: "Rulers and elders of the people! If we are being called to account today for an act of kindness shown to a man who was lame and are being asked how he was healed, then know this, you and all the people of Israel: It is by the name of Jesus Christ of Nazareth, whom you crucified but whom God raised from the dead, that this man stands before you healed. Jesus is

"'the stone you builders rejected,
which has become the cornerstone.'

Salvation is found in no one else, for there is no other name under heaven given to mankind by which we must be saved."

When they saw the courage of Peter and John and realized that they were unschooled, ordinary men, they were astonished and they took note that these men had been with Jesus. (Acts 4:7–13)

The marks of genuine followers of Jesus involved courage and boldness. The hired hand runs when serious trouble comes:

> I am the good shepherd. The good shepherd lays down his life for the sheep. He who is a hired hand and not a shepherd, who does not own the sheep, sees the wolf coming and leaves the sheep and flees, and the wolf snatches them and scatters them. He flees because he is a hired hand and cares nothing for the sheep. (John 10:11–13 ESV)

The wolves came and will come. In Acts 20:29–31 Paul bluntly says:

> I know that after my departure fierce wolves will come in among you, not sparing the flock; and from among your own selves will arise men speaking twisted things, to draw away the disciples after them. Therefore be alert, remembering that for three years I did not cease night or day to admonish every one with tears. (ESV)

"Fierce" has the sense of weight, stress, and violence. There will be stressful times and in places that may even lead to violence. This is not a once-in-a-disciple's-lifetime event. It will regularly come like a change in season. It will come from without and within the church. How will we handle this stress? At tough times, I have seen so-called spiritual leaders flee like hired hands. I have also seen others stand their ground on the "day of evil" (Ephesians 6:13).

On the boat in the middle of the Sea of Galilee under severe stress from the wind and waves, Jesus emphatically calls on his disciples to take courage.

> He saw the disciples straining at the oars, because the wind was against them. Shortly before dawn he went out to them, walking on the lake. He was about to pass by them, but when they saw him walking on the lake, they thought he was a ghost. They cried out, because they all saw him and were terrified.

Immediately he spoke to them and said, *"Take courage!* It is I. Don't be afraid." Then he climbed into the boat with them, and the wind died down. (Mark 6:48–51, emphasis added)

So courage is there, but it is also something we take up for the spiritual warfare that is inevitable in God's kingdom. There are times when people, in reaction to an overemphasis on one metaphor for God's kingdom, shift to another. Usually there is a push to move from the military metaphor to the family metaphor. It is "safer." Sometimes we beat our swords into plowshares (Isaiah 2:4), and sometimes we beat our plowshares into swords (Joel 3:10). But we are not meant to be swinging like a pendulum on the metaphors of the church. They are all applicable and necessary for God's people at all times. We do need to make sure we keep them all in balance, using them all. The metaphors of the family and the soldier can coexist.

Courage is the conditional promise to Joshua given from the Lord as the necessary response of the covenantal relationship.

I will never leave you nor forsake you. Be strong and courageous, because you will lead these people to inherit the land I swore to their ancestors to give them.

Be strong and very courageous. Be careful to obey all the law my servant Moses gave you....

Have I not commanded you? Be strong and courageous. Do not be afraid; do not be discouraged, for the LORD your God will be with you wherever you go." (Joshua 1:5–7, 9)

Courage is not a natural state. It is something we must take up and put on. It is the opposite of being victims. It means we are not in a "safe place," but somewhere that is dangerous to our emotional and possibly physical wellbeing. And we take courage as disciples of Jesus, which is how he wants us to respond.

We live in a culture that is reluctant to hold up the one who has had courage, and instead prefers to focus on the perceived victims. There was an interesting story published on April 7, 2003 by the *WSJ* about an incident in the Iraq War.

When American troops were attacked on April 7 on a road to Baghdad, a battle broke out at an intersection called "Objective Curly." Eighty US soldiers, expecting little resistance, were met by 300 well-armed Iraqi and Syrian fighters. Grenades and bullets flew for eight hours.

The US counterattack killed an estimated 200 enemy fighters, according to the commanding officer who oversaw the battle. The American team had never trained or fought together, but all its men got out alive. The team was headed by Capt. Harry Alexander Hornbuckle, a 29-year-old staff officer who had never been in combat before. He was later awarded the Bronze Star, with a V for valor, for his efforts that day. Capt. Hornbuckle's name has never appeared in a newspaper or on television. He has received no book deals, no movie offers, no trips to Disneyland. In September, when he went to see his parents in Tifton, GA, his mother called the local Holiday Inn and asked the manager to put her son's name—he goes by Zan—on the hotel marquee. That has been his most public recognition so far. He is one of several soldiers who rose to extraordinary heights on the battlefield in Iraq, received honors from the military and returned home to anonymity.

Instead, the best-known soldier of the Iraq War is Jessica Lynch, who suffered broken bones and other injuries when her maintenance convoy was attacked. She was rescued from an Iraqi hospital a week later. The rescue and initial reports—later discredited—that the 19-year-old had survived bullet and stab wounds and continued fighting helped make her a celebrity. Stores in her hometown of Palestine, WV, sold T-shirts with her name on them. Volunteers planted a new garden in front of her house. Alfred A. Knopf, the publishing house, signed her to a $1 million book deal. *Saving Jessica Lynch,* a TV movie about her plight, was broadcast Sunday.

The writer's reason for such a crisis is that since the Vietnam War, victims are celebrated rather than aggressors. According to his commander, Captain Hornbuckle "took a chaotic situation and got it under control." He also kept all his men alive while devastating the enemy.

The point of this illustration is not to highlight war and death. It is to make sure we highlight those who have stood with courage, rather than just focusing on angry victims.

What are some areas where courage is needed?

First is courage to take a stand on God's word. And our courage needs to be seen by others. One striking example is Nehemiah 6:

> Now when I went into the house of Shemaiah the son of Delaiah, son of Mehetabel, who was confined to his home, he said, "Let us meet together in the house of God, within the temple. Let us close the doors of the temple, for they are coming to kill you. They are coming to kill you by night." But I said, "Should such a man as I run away? And what man such as I could go into the temple and live? I will not go in." And I understood and saw that God had not sent him, but he had pronounced the prophecy against me because Tobiah and Sanballat had hired him. For this purpose he was hired, that I should be afraid and act in this way and sin, and so they could give me a bad name in order to taunt me. Remember Tobiah and Sanballat, O my God, according to these things that they did, and also the prophetess Noadiah and the rest of the prophets who wanted to make me afraid. (Nehemiah 6:10–14 ESV)

The pressure was placed on Nehemiah to lay low, to hide out. He would not have a bit of it. *But I said, "Should such a man as I run away?"* Many, including the prophetess Noadiah, (little is known of her) encouraged Nehemiah to give in to fear and hide. But there are times to "man up." When stressful times hit, it is a time "to run to the fight and hold each other tight." As with the Apostle Paul, there must be the urge to walk into the amphitheater in Ephesus and face the crowd.

Second, spiritual leaders are on the offensive. If the gates of Hades cannot stand against the kingdom of God, it implies that we are on the attack, not on the defensive. More mistakes will be made if that is our mindset. It might make us jump into a pit with a lion on a snowy day. And of course, the aggressors are not always the "bad guys" in the eyes of God. Like David's mighty men, when all others are fleeing, they take their stand.

Spiritual leaders should always have a long-term perspective. Many times the immediate crisis that hits us makes us want to defend ourselves against whatever charge is brought against us. But defensiveness is never a great quality for a spiritual leader or any disciple. Time will sort out most things. We should always make some effort to clarify, but not give in to fretting or be controlled by worry. Worry leads to the wrong outcome: "Refrain from anger and turn from wrath; do not fret—it leads only to evil" (Psalm 37:8). One needs to be concerned about the outcome of our lives and not just a snapshot. God always comes through. And if our eyes are on him who sits on the throne, God will not abandon us. We may open our eyes and be in heaven, but he always leads us in triumph.

Over the years, I have been criticized more times than I can count. Usually it was tied to leading with courage and taking a stand that rubbed people the wrong way. There is a certain scorn to being called "old school." It is not true that this didn't bother me or keep me up late at night replaying the comments and rebuttals over and over again. But as I sailed past forty, my ability to see things close up diminished more quickly than my ability to see things at a distance. Peter wrote in one of the last letters in the New Testament encouraging us to set our vision not on the immediate, but on the everlasting and to work on our character, not the issue of the moment. Working on our faith and character need to be our battles, not the present crisis. "For whoever lacks these qualities is so nearsighted that he is blind, having forgotten that he was cleansed from his former sins" (2 Peter 1:9 ESV). As we age, we are meant to remember that God has always come through and will continue to protect and guard us as he always has.

We are soldiers in the army.
We have to fight, although we have to cry.
We have to hold up the bloodstained banner.
We have to hold it up until we die!

My father was a soldier, oh yes!
He had his hand on the gospel plow.
But one day he got old;
he couldn't fight anymore.
He said, "I'll stand here and fight anyhow."

· Chapter Twelve ·

Committed to God's Word

I charge you in the presence of God and of Christ Jesus, who is to judge the living and the dead, and by his appearing and his kingdom: preach the word; be ready in season and out of season; reprove, rebuke, and exhort, with complete patience and teaching. For the time is coming when people will not endure sound teaching, but having itching ears they will accumulate for themselves teachers to suit their own passions, and will turn away from listening to the truth and wander off into myths. (2 Timothy 4:1–4 ESV)

Let the word of Christ dwell in you richly, teaching and admonishing one another in all wisdom, singing psalms and hymns and spiritual songs, with thankfulness in your hearts to God. (Colossians 3:16 ESV)

Forever, O LORD, your word
    is firmly fixed in the heavens.
Your faithfulness endures to all generations;
    you have established the earth, and it stands
fast. (Psalm 119:89–90 ESV)

There are many other scriptures that could be listed emphasizing the centrality of basing our lives, including spiritual leadership, on the inspired word of God. God's word does not change with the seasons. We use it in season and out, not dependent on the cultural times or what is acceptable. God's word is not seasonal, and its unchangeability is tied metaphorically, as the psalmist writes, to the heavens. It is firmly fixed there.

I live in Australia and always enjoy leaving the metropolitan areas to be able to see the vastness of the heavens. I look up and see the same stars that Abraham saw. His descendants would be like the vastness of the stars in the sky (Genesis 15:5). I see the same stars that Moses saw when he was given God's Law. I see the same stars as David, and all the prophets. The same stars that Jesus saw while he lived on the earth, and Paul saw as he traveled the Roman Empire. They have not changed! These stars, as the psalmist writes, are a visible metaphor of God's commandments for us. They are meant to remind us of God's word that is unchanging.

It seems so strange that we on the planet can think we can change God's word here, as if we are the center of the universe. We can make new commandments about life ("my truth") as if we are the creators of who we are and how we were made to function. In each hemisphere, there is a guiding star that determines the direction of north and south. The North Star is pointed to by two stars in the Big Dipper that point to the last star in the tail of the Little Dipper (Polaris). They point to true north.

In the southern hemisphere, there are two pointer stars that direct you to the Southern Cross. If you draw an imaginary line from the top of the cross to the bottom and extend it four and a half times and drop a vertical line from that point, that will be South Celestial Pole, due south. So north or south, the stars can direct us. And in the southern hemisphere, it is comforting that the constellation reminds us of the cross. That which guides us in every area of our life is meant to be the gospel, centered on the cross.

In the musical *Les Misérables* (based on Victor Hugo's novel), one song, "Stars," speaks of this same guidance as a metaphor of God's word. The songwriter tells us that if we follow the way of the Law, we will know our way in the dark as the stars keep watch like sentinels and fill the darkness with light. One line of the song is: "Those who follow the path of the righteous shall have their reward."

God's word stands firm. It is a firm foundation that cannot be moved or changed (Ephesians 2:20). And if we build our lives on God's word and obeying it, we build a spiritual house that will not collapse:

> "Therefore everyone who hears these words of mine and puts them into practice is like a wise man who built his house on the rock. The rain came down, the streams rose, and the winds blew and beat against that house; yet it did not fall, because it had its foundation on the rock. But everyone who hears these words of mine and does not put them into practice is like a foolish man who built his house on sand." (Matthew 7:24–26)

Paul commands us in Colossians 3:16, using the imperative tense, to let the word of God dwell in us richly as we teach and admonish one another. To dwell richly is from a Greek word, πλουσίωςα, pertaining to that which exists in a large amount, with the implication of its being valuable. If God's word is better than gold, than using God's word richly means using it abundantly. We use it to teach and admonish, to give knowledge that leads to a change in heart and behavior.

Paul writes to the Romans and uses the same language in Romans 15:14: "I myself am convinced, my brothers and sisters, that you yourselves are full of goodness, filled with knowledge and competent to instruct one another."

Knowledge is God's word. To instruct (*nouetheo*, "admonish") is putting it on our heart and into practice as we spiritually lead. So head knowledge is connected by discipling to our heart, which controls our will and actions.

The biblical expectation from those who preach is that they preach God's word in season and out. Anecdotal sermons, sermons built around an illustration, narcissistic sermons in which the preacher just talks about his life as if that is what we came to hear, emotional little stories that we then transfer over to God, or preaching like a commentary reads, all are not using God's word "richly."

Listening attentively and compassionately accompany using God's word as we lead and teach others. Without listening, we are unable to clearly identify what scriptures would be useful. Without compassion and expressing care, we make it difficult for those we address to listen. Jesus showed both compassion and strong direction to his disciples. And his compassion determined how strongly he addressed his listeners: to the broken, gently; to the arrogant, with strength and directness, but all coming from love.

Throughout biblical times and church history, those following God would let his word be their guiding light on a daily basis. David would rise in the night and meditate on God's word. Christians through the centuries made it a daily practice to start the day reading and meditating on the Scriptures to set their minds on things above before they had to direct their thoughts and actions on things below. The Benedictine Rule for monastic life coined the phrase "Prime Time," which started early in the morning when they focused on God's word and prayer. One does not outgrow this need, this taking up the cross daily in one's life. There seems to be a danger, as we mature in Christ, to think we are beyond this daily need, and that spiritual disciplines are only for the young and not for those who have outgrown this simple practice.

Here are some practical points to consider.

First, keeping a journal of your time with God and his word each day has been proven very helpful over church history. It does several things: 1. If we date each entry, then it gently reminds us how consistent we have been. 2. The insights we gain from the Scriptures will be a source of many a lesson to others. The Spirit can direct us to meet needs that we are not even aware of. He knows the hearts of those we lead and what they need. 3. Preparing a lesson is different from having a personal quiet time. Our perspective changes when we read the Word to be a mirror to our own life, not the lives we plan to address. Thus, getting our own heart right is the first step in preaching powerfully with zeal and integrity. And this leads to lessons and input that come from a heart that is regularly listening to God's word and speaking with honest conviction and passion.

Second, work at keeping your heart soft to God's word. There are several metaphors the Scriptures use to help us maintain a soft heart. One such is breaking up unplowed ground in our lives.

> This is what the LORD says to the people of Judah and to Jerusalem:
>> "Break up your unplowed ground
>> and do not sow among thorns." (Jeremiah 4:3)

> "Sow righteousness for yourselves,
>> reap the fruit of unfailing love,
> and break up your unplowed ground;
>> for it is time to seek the LORD,
> until he comes
>> and showers his righteousness on you."
> (Hosea 10:12)

> Haughty eyes and a proud heart—
>> the unplowed field of the wicked—produce
>> sin. (Proverbs 21:4)

One of the reasons we continue to read Scripture is the knowledge that at our best, we still are far from the righteousness of God. Apart from Christ, there is no one righteous, no not one (Romans 3). The sanctification process never ends. Even on our deathbeds, there will be a need to deal with our hearts. If you are experiencing spiritual dryness, think about areas in your life that either need revisiting or need exploring. It would be wise, according to the Proverbs, to get outside eyes, those you and others think are wise, to ask them to give you input in areas where you might be blind from self-deceit. Look for those whose "outcome of their lives" reflects spiritual values. And the most tender spots that cause an emotional reaction need the washing of the Word from the great Physician.

The second metaphor is the graphic image of having uncircumcised ears and uncircumcised hearts. "The uncircumcised" was a pejorative term for Israel's enemies: "uncircumcised Philistines." Jeremiah will then apply it to the people of Judah!

> To whom shall I speak and give warning,
>   that they may hear?
> Behold, their ears are uncircumcised,
>   they cannot listen;
> behold, the word of the LORD is to them an object of scorn;
>   they take no pleasure in it.
> Therefore I am full of the wrath of the LORD;
>   I am weary of holding it in. (Jeremiah 6:10–11a ESV)

Stephen in his sermon at his trial leading to his stoning used the same metaphor, which led to their outrage: "You stiff-necked people! Your hearts and ears are still uncircumcised. You are just like your ancestors: You always resist the Holy Spirit!" (Acts 7:51).

Our ears need to be metaphorically cut! Our hearts need to be cut!

> Egypt, Judah, Edom, Ammon, Moab and all who live in the wilderness in distant places. For all these nations are really uncircumcised, and even the whole house of Israel is uncircumcised in heart. (Jeremiah 9:26)

Few like to be compared to others, but to be compared to our enemies makes most flinch. The word of God is meant to cut. We are meant to have our ears and hearts cut. Our ears, so we can more clearly hear what God is saying. Faith comes from hearing the word of God. That is why biblical preaching is so needed. If you are spending more time on the visual that people see rather than speaking to their ears, it may be time to readjust your time and work more on what you will say.

It is a fact that as we age, our hearing deteriorates, a process medically called presbycusis. There are several factors that cause this, often a hardening of the parts of the ear that control hearing. It should be a warning as we age to make sure we are listening to God's word. Are we getting sentimentally soft as we age? Are we weary of the spiritual warfare that never ends even as we age? People can be hardened into positions both left and right. But it is God's word that gives us the balance we need, and our ears are the part of our anatomy that controls our balance. So one must work hard on listening to God.

If it has been a long time since you have been cut by the Scriptures, don't blame the messengers, but look to your own heart. It is meant to be a painful yet healthy process!

There are times, even among God's people, when it is hard to find others who have this deeply felt conviction about the Scriptures. The Scriptures talk of those who "tremble" at God's word.

> "Has not my hand made all these things,
>   and so they came into being?"
>   declares the LORD.

> "These are the ones I look on with favor:
>   those who are humble and contrite in spirit,
>   and who tremble at my word. (Isaiah 66:2)

> "For they have taken some of their daughters to be wives for themselves and for their sons, so that the holy race has mixed itself with the peoples of the lands. And in this faithlessness the hand of the officials and chief men has been foremost." As soon as I heard this, I tore my garment and my cloak and pulled hair from my head and beard and sat appalled. Then all who trembled at the words of the God of Israel, because of the faithlessness of the returned exiles, gathered around me while I sat appalled until the evening sacrifice. And at the evening sacrifice I rose from my fasting, with my garment and my cloak torn, and fell upon my knees and spread out my hands to the LORD my God, saying:
> "O my God, I am ashamed and blush to lift my face

to you, my God, for our iniquities have risen higher than our heads, and our guilt has mounted up to the heavens." (Ezra 9:2-6)

Ezra trembled not at his own sin, but the corporate sin of God's people, as the people had yoked themselves with unbelievers. When was the last time you trembled thinking about the state of God's people?

Our cultures will attempt to make us feel insecure about our biblical values, characterizing us as bigoted and ignorant. But on the other hand, being a man or woman faithful to God's word gives us eternal security. Most are aware of Jesus' admonishment that if we choose to be his disciples, we should not be ashamed. "Whoever is ashamed of me and my words, the Son of Man be ashamed of them when he comes in his glory and in the glory of the Father and of the holy angels" (Luke 9:26). Most read this challenge and focus on not being ashamed of Jesus, but it is not just Jesus that is listed as a possible source of embarrassment. We are not to be ashamed of his words. We are not to be embarrassed by those who seek to shame us, but to have the fire within our bellies that cannot but speak and say what God wants proclaimed.

> If I say, "I will not mention him,
>   or speak any more in his name,"
> there is in my heart as it were a burning fire
>   shut up in my bones,
> and I am weary with holding it in,
>   *and I cannot* (Jeremiah 20:9, emphasis added).

God's word cannot be chained, so says the chained Apostle Paul in 2 Timothy 2:8b-9: "This is my gospel, for which I am suffering even to the point of being chained like a criminal. But God's word is not chained" Not chained could be translated today as "not canceled." It cannot be stopped! God laughs at such attempts. Let us laugh with him!

· Chapter Thirteen ·

Leaders Preach Repentance

> Now after John was arrested, Jesus came into Galilee, proclaiming the gospel of God, and saying, "The time is fulfilled, and the kingdom of God is at hand; repent and believe in the gospel."
>
> Passing alongside the Sea of Galilee, he saw Simon and Andrew the brother of Simon casting a net into the sea, for they were fishermen. And Jesus said to them, "Follow me, and I will make you become fishers of men." (Mark 1:14–17 ESV)

Jesus began his ministry following the arrest of John the Baptist (who also preached repentance), proclaiming the good news of God, that the time was right, and the call was to repentance and faith in this good news. He then begins to call his disciples to follow him. Following him is preaching the same message. It is the final charge from Peter after his Pentecostal sermon in Acts 2:38 calling them all to repent and be baptized in Jesus' name.

Much has been written about repentance, *metanoia*, meaning a new mind, a change in direction, and not just a sorrowful emotion but godly sorrow (versus worldly sorrow) leading to repentance (2 Corinthians 7:10). For those early disciples, fishing for men meant bringing men and women to a change of mind and heart shown in their actions (Acts 26:20).

But so-called spiritual leaders throughout the Old Testament and New Testament failed to proclaim God's expectation. Like

Aaron listening to the people while Moses is on the mountain getting the Ten Commandments and doing what the people were demanding rather than calling them to repentance. And like the false prophets and priests Jeremiah rebuked who gave the people what they wanted, not what they needed.

> "For from the least to the greatest of them,
>   everyone is greedy for unjust gain;
> and from prophet to priest,
>   everyone deals falsely.
> They have healed the wound of my people lightly,
>   saying, 'Peace, peace,'
>   when there is no peace.
> Were they ashamed when they committed abomination?
>   No, they were not at all ashamed;
>   they did not know how to blush." (Jeremiah 6:13–15 ESV)

Goodhearted people do not go to church to hear what they want to hear, but what they need to hear. They long for healthy preaching, not sugary fluff. And while they might enjoy pleasant and clever preaching for a while, eventually they want solid food.

Look how God sees the people of Judah:

> An appalling and horrible thing
>   has happened in the land:
> the prophets prophesy falsely,
>   and the priests rule at their direction;
> my people love to have it so,
>   but what will you do when the end comes?
> (Jeremiah 5:30–31 ESV)

But, really, what will they do in the end? Yes, you can preach what people want to hear, take surveys to lead them where they want to go, but if you believe the Scriptures, what indeed will they do at judgment? And what accountability will God hold the leaders to who allow that to happen? They will be judged by an even stricter standard.

The last book of the Old Testament sets the stage for the New Testament. The last words are verses of hope but also of devastation.

> "Behold, I will send you Elijah the prophet before the great and awesome day of the LORD comes. And he will turn the hearts of fathers to their children and the hearts of children to their fathers, lest I come and strike the land with a decree of utter destruction." (Malachi 4:5–6 ESV)

Where were the people of God, then, at the close of the Old Testament? They had dreamed of Zion in their Babylonian captivity. They had returned to the promised land. All was exciting and exhilarating. But after time, they began to slip again, so common of God's people. Let's look at a few points, three areas where God through Malachi challenges his people.

First, there is a loss of fear, honor, and respect toward God. Malachi challenges them with that charge of disrespect, and they respond with, "How have we done this? Give us an example." God says it is:

> "By offering polluted food upon my altar. But you say, 'How have we polluted you?' By saying that the LORD's table may be despised. When you offer blind animals in sacrifice, is that not evil? And when you offer those that are lame or sick, is that not evil? Present that to your governor; will he accept you or show you favor? says the LORD of hosts." (Malachi 1:7–8 ESV)

The people were offering not their best as prescribed by God, but their worst. Try doing that with the governor, he says! In other words, the governor would not let you get away with that.

Most read this and take it personally: Yes, one must give God the best, the first fruits, and the best unblemished sacrifices. But the charge is not really addressed to the people, for it is the priests who make the offering for the people. God says it is "you,

O priests, who despise my name" (v. 6). The people bring the offerings, but the priest is in charge of the actual sacrifice. The leaders, the priests, are letting the people bring the worst, the leftovers, and not the best to God. But it is their job to challenge the people who are giving less than their best to God.

I am sure you can imagine the priest thinking, *Well, at least they are giving something. We should commend them for the little effort that they do make.* Like times when some churches are thankful that at least people come at Christmas and Easter. *At least we are getting a tithe of something, but if we push them, we may get nothing. We want to make the whole following God thing more pleasant for them, more attractive. How can making it more demanding really help to get our numbers up at the sacrifices? Let's offer them honey, not vinegar.*

Many spiritual leaders ask the wrong questions of the wrong people. The one you should be addressing is God, and what you should stress is his expectations. And if everyone is displeased with you, but God is pleased with you, that is what really counts. This is not only for our own personal good, but the good of those we serve. What does God think of those who give him less than the best? "Cursed be the cheat who has a male in his flock, and vows it, and yet sacrifices to the Lord what is blemished. For I am a great King, says the Lord of hosts, and my name will be feared among the nations" (Malachi 1:14 ESV). Spiritual leaders are not people-pleasers, but are controlled by the demands of God. They fear God and are fearful of God's response to the people they lead. If they are cheating God (his words), we must address that for their sake.

Look at the outcome of what the people think of the priests in Malachi who are letting them get away with their lack of commitment and trust:

> "For the lips of a priest should guard knowledge, and people should seek instruction from his mouth, for he is the messenger of the LORD of hosts. But you have turned aside from the way. You have caused many to stumble by your instruction. You have corrupted the

covenant of Levi, says the LORD of hosts, and so I make you despised and abased before all the people, inasmuch as you do not keep my ways but show partiality in your instruction." (Malachi 2:7–9 ESV)

Despised and abased (ESV) and *despised and humiliated* (NIV) is how the people will view their leadership. It is how they are depicted in much of literature and film. Of course, the real opinion that counts is what God thinks of them. And God shares the people's opinion; in fact, he is putting those thoughts in their minds. Good parents are very concerned that their children are respectful. And if it is not taught and expected, they, too, are disrespected by their children.

Second, the marriages and families are affected, the foundational building blocks of God's people.

And this second thing you do. You cover the LORD'S altar with tears, with weeping and groaning because he no longer regards the offering or accepts it with favor from your hand. But you say, "Why does he not?" Because the LORD was witness between you and the wife of your youth, to whom you have been faithless, though she is your companion and your wife by covenant. Did he not make them one, with a portion of the Spirit in their union? And what was the one God seeking? Godly offspring. So guard yourselves in your spirit, and let none of you be faithless to the wife of your youth. "For the man who does not love his wife but divorces her, says the LORD, the God of Israel, covers his garment with violence, says the LORD of hosts. So guard yourselves in your spirit, and do not be faithless." (Malachi 2:13–16 ESV)

Two areas that spiritual leadership needs to protect and nurture are marriage and family. God's people, then as well as now, too often think they are exceptions that allow the bending of God's standards for marriage.

God's word through Moses was very clear:

> When the LORD your God gives them over to you, and you defeat them, then you must devote them to complete destruction. You shall make no covenant with them and show no mercy to them. You shall not intermarry with them, giving your daughters to their sons or taking their daughters for your sons, for they would turn away your sons from following me, to serve other gods. Then the anger of the LORD would be kindled against you, and he would destroy you quickly. (Deuteronomy 7:2–4 ESV)

This seems pretty clear even to the simple. Yet emotions and arrogance can cloud one's judgment. Even the wisest can rationalize their disobedience, even if you are the smartest person around as Solomon was.

> Now King Solomon loved many foreign women, along with the daughter of Pharaoh: Moabite, Ammonite, Edomite, Sidonian, and Hittite women, from the nations concerning which the LORD had said to the people of Israel, "You shall not enter into marriage with them, neither shall they with you, for surely they will turn away your heart after their gods." Solomon clung to these in love. He had 700 wives, who were princesses, and 300 concubines. And his wives turned away his heart. For when Solomon was old his wives turned away his heart after other gods, and his heart was not wholly true to the LORD his God, as was the heart of David his father. (1 Kings 11:1–4 ESV)

Solomon, unlike his father, was not a warrior. He didn't conquer the enemies around God's people, he just made treaties sealed by him taking a princess of that country. It all made sense and avoided painful conflict. Yet what sounded so reasonable ended with these very women turning his heart away from God.

Not turned totally, but not wholly true to the Lord. Isn't that the language people use? We're not leaving God, but following our heart.

The other situation that was undermining the foundation of Israel was divorce. The religious leaders asked Jesus if it was right to divorce your wife for any reason. "And Pharisees came up to him and tested him by asking, 'Is it lawful to divorce one's wife for any cause?'" (Matthew 19:3 ESV). The very question implies that divorce was common. Jesus responded with a very high standard for marriage. It was so high that even his disciples responded that maybe it was better not to marry at all.

As a young disciple, the very idea that divorce would become common in the church was unthinkable. Leaders used to, perhaps arrogantly, say, "There is no divorce in our movement." Well, no one says that anymore! But spiritual leadership cannot lower the standards because divorce has become accepted. Again, spiritual leadership is resolved to keep God's word even when it hurts. How can evangelicals in the US have a higher divorce rate than even atheists? The compromises have opened the floodgate to an undermined church. No one wants to talk about it lest they end up like John the Baptist (figuratively). After all, what was he arrested for?

The third call to repentance in Malachi addresses their giving.

> "For I the LORD do not change; therefore you, O children of Jacob, are not consumed. From the days of your fathers you have turned aside from my statutes and have not kept them. Return to me, and I will return to you, says the LORD of hosts. But you say, 'How shall we return?' Will man rob God? Yet you are robbing me. But you say, 'How have we robbed you?' In your tithes and contributions." (Malachi 3:6–8 ESV)

As preachers have often said, the heart strings and the purse strings are connected. Again, spiritual leadership will not back away from preaching about it and expecting people to give. I do not think spiritual leadership is checking up through adminis-trators what the people are personally giving. But it is right to address it on a personal level and ask if one is giving sacrificially. Again, it is leadership that expects the best from God's people. Robbing God does not sound like an inconsequential act. And if we care for the sheep, there are no areas that are off limits.

Repentance is to be preached and expected. Paul defends the content of his preaching in Acts 26:19-21:

> "Therefore, O King Agrippa, I was not disobedient to the heavenly vision, but declared first to those in Da-mascus, then in Jerusalem and throughout all the re-gion of Judea, and also to the Gentiles, that they should repent and turn to God, performing deeds in keeping with their repentance. For this reason the Jews seized me in the temple and tried to kill me." (ESV)

What hopefully marks our leadership is exactly the same. We need to exercise that kind of leadership and have God's expec-tations. And as we preach repentance, expect serious pushback from those who have drifted in their convictions.

Let us be spiritual leaders that lead as God expects, no matter what the consequences.

· Chapter Fourteen ·

Spiritual Leadership in the Home

Submit to one another out of reverence for Christ.

Wives, submit yourselves to your own husbands as you do to the Lord. For the husband is the head of the wife as Christ is the head of the church, his body, of which he is the Savior. Now as the church submits to Christ, so also wives should submit to their husbands in everything.

Husbands, love your wives, just as Christ loved the church and gave himself up for her to make her holy, cleansing her by the washing with water through the word, and to present her to himself as a radiant church, without stain or wrinkle or any other blemish, but holy and blameless. In this same way, husbands ought to love their wives as their own bodies. He who loves his wife loves himself. After all, no one ever hated their own body, but they feed and care for their body, just as Christ does the church— for we are members of his body. "For this reason a man will leave his father and mother and be united to his wife, and the two will become one flesh." This is a profound mystery—but I am talking about Christ and the church. However, each one of you also must love his wife as he loves himself, and the wife must respect her husband.

Children, obey your parents in the Lord, for this is right. "Honor your father and mother"—which is the first commandment with a promise— "so that it may go well with you and that you may enjoy long life on the earth."

Fathers, do not exasperate your children; instead, bring them up in the training and instruction of the Lord. (Ephesians 5:21–6:4)

The two scriptures in Ephesians 5:21 and 22 are meant to go together. They are not in contradiction, but rather explain how God intends families to live together in harmony. No family thrives without mutual submission in ways too numerous to list. But spiritual leadership is clearly mandated in the family. There has been much discussion in Western cultures as the secular values of leadership have undermined biblical values in many areas.

I have been blessed with a very strong spiritual woman as my wife, and together we raised three very strong spiritual daughters. They have all married strong spiritual men, and God has blessed them, and my wife and me, with ten grandchildren.

We are all still a work in progress, but there are some suggestions and principles from my life experience that have so far helped our family stay strong in the Lord. It is the legacy I most treasure and pray for daily. As an early riser, I rarely get out of bed before spending time going through my family specifically, name by name. I pray for each grandchild to become a disciple and stay a strong disciple, and pray that one day they would marry a strong disciple. I emphasize "strong," knowing all the battles and struggles that test our faith and perseverance. I pray for unity and spiritual leadership for all the fathers and mothers. I know that only by God's grace and power can those blessings come to our family.

Let's consider some principles that I believe are crucial.

First, spiritual leadership always works at unity, and particularly in the family, unity between a husband and wife. If there is one thing I have found crucial for families to function in a healthy spiritual way, it is this. The psalmist David describes unity in songs of ascent:

How good and pleasant it is
    when God's people live together in unity!
It is like precious oil poured on the head,
    running down on the beard,
running down on Aaron's beard,
    down on the collar of his robe.
It is as if the dew of Hermon
    were falling on Mount Zion.
For there the LORD bestows his blessing,
    even life forevermore. (Psalm 133:1–3)

David's description is not just about feel-good moments. It is in the ambience of such a setting of unity that the Lord "bestows his blessing, even life forevermore." The ESV more literally states: "For there the Lord has commanded the blessing, life forevermore." It is like heavy dew at Israel's highest mountain, dampening dry, arid Jerusalem.

In Genesis 1, God's work of creation is described concerning mankind:

So God created man in his own image,
    in the image of God he created him;
    male and female he created them. (Genesis 1:27 ESV)

The world where the original readers of Genesis lived was a world filled with the images of gods. The thoughtful worshippers of those images would know that the images were not really their gods. They just represented their deities so their eyes could visualize and enhance their worship. But in Genesis 1, the image of God would be man. More specifically, his image would be a combination of man and woman together. Genesis 1 is followed in the next chapter by God dividing man into male and female parts. But God's image is a combination of both in verse 27, where using Hebrew parallelism, in which the words of two or more lines of text are directly related in some way, the singular man is then listed as male and female in the next line.

So the clearest image of God on earth will be a male and

female united through God. It is no wonder that our marriages and sexuality are so attacked by the evil one, who wants to destroy that image of God. Every time Satan sees a spiritual couple united, he sees this image. So his attack on marriage is an attack on the healthy image of God on earth. And his success is seen in the many distorted images of God present in our world today.

As this relates to the family, the unity of husband and wife will be the clearest image of God our children will see in their homes. If the parents are united under God, then the children more likely will see and have a healthy image of God. If the parents aren't united, even though they are individually committed to God, then the children will have a distorted, confused image of God.

So parents should always be working on their unity, even if it means less attention to their children, for the sake of their children.

Second, spiritual leadership in the home instills a mission mindedness that is shared by all members of the household. There is relatively little said directly in the New Testament concerning marriage and raising children. What is centered on in the New Testament is how to live a disciple's life. Thus, if we stress living as disciples, this affects and changes our homes. All disciples of Jesus are by definition mission minded. To follow Jesus is to follow him in his mission to seek and save the lost.

So, effective spiritual leadership is always directing the family outward to change the world rather than letting the world change them.

Michael Crichton in his book *The Lost World* (on which the movie *Jurassic Park* is based) writes of the "line of chaos:"

> But even more important is the way complex systems seem to strike a balance between the need for order and the imperative to change. Complex systems tend to locate themselves at a place we call "the edge of chaos." We imagine the edge of chaos as a place where there is enough innovation to keep a

living system vibrant, and enough stability to keep it from collapsing into anarchy. It is a zone of conflict and upheaval, where the old and the new are constantly at war. Finding the balance point must be a delicate matter—if a living system drifts too close, it risks falling over into incoherence and dissolution; but if the system moves too far away from the edge, it becomes rigid, frozen, totalitarian. Both conditions lead to extinction. Too much change is as destructive as too little. Only at the edge of chaos can complex systems flourish... And, by implication, extinction is the inevitable result of one or the other strategy—too much change, or too little.

Most life lives along this edge, where the jungle meets the desert, where reefs meet the ocean. If one learns to live along that edge, there is much creative and colorful life. Parents need to teach and train their children to live along this edge.

Jesus' prayer for his disciples in John 17 relates to this charge to his disciples: "My prayer is not that you take them out of the world but that you protect them from the evil one. They are not of the world, even as I am not of it. Sanctify them by the truth; your word is truth. As you sent me into the world, I have sent them into the world" (vv. 15-18).

If I send them to "Christian" universities to keep them safe, but they never learn how to make disciples, have I overprotected them and made them evangelistically sterile? Do we provide too few godly boundaries, endangering them from being entrapped by the world? This is the tough job of spiritual leadership.

Third, spiritual leadership teaches and practices servant-hood, not entitlement, in the family. Parents should train their children to be caregivers to the many who have not had the blessings of coming from a Christian household. They should demonstrate servanthood in their parenting and reinforce it as Jesus did when he washed his disciples' feet: "If I then, your Lord and Teacher, have washed your feet, you also ought to wash one another's feet. For I have given you an example, that you also should do just as I have done to you" (John 13:14-15 ESV). We convey that if we, your parents, serve you, you also must learn this practice and demonstrate it to others.

A definition of entitlement as it relates to the family is this: the belief that one is inherently deserving of privileges or special treatment. Most children naturally have some of these qualities, being part of a family and having been raised by parents who give so much. A big job of parenting, however, is training them to learn the simple teaching of Jesus:

> In all things I have shown you that by working hard in this way we must help the weak and remember the words of the Lord Jesus, how he himself said, "It is more blessed to give than to receive." (Acts 20:35 ESV)

Some simple things we taught in our family were:

- Greet visitors to our home, and welcome them with good eye contact and offer them a drink.

- In restaurants, again, make eye contact with the server and show some respect for them as people.

- At teen events and church services, go up to the visitors and meet them, especially other teens; do not be cliquish with your friends, but invite visitors into your circle.

- When people come to visit church, think of questions to ask them about their lives. If they are visiting from other churches, ask about their ministries.

- At the table, always show appreciation for the food prepared and be willing to at least taste what is served. And if the food is not to your liking, still give a pleasant response.

Fourth, be parents and spiritual leaders in the home with a very high level of integrity. Integrity means wholeness, oneness: What you are on the outside is what you are on the inside. Jesus is well aware that people can play the religious game, being one way publicly and another way privately. In Matthew 7, the test is the fruit of their lives, the outcome of their lives.

> "Beware of false prophets, who come to you in sheep's clothing but inwardly are ravenous wolves. You will recognize them by their fruits. Are grapes gathered from thornbushes, or figs from thistles? So, every healthy tree bears good fruit, but the diseased tree bears bad fruit. A healthy tree cannot bear bad fruit, nor can a diseased tree bear good fruit. Every tree that does not bear good fruit is cut down and thrown into the fire. Thus you will recognize them by their fruits.
> "Not everyone who says to me, 'Lord, Lord,' will enter the kingdom of heaven, but the one who does the will of my Father who is in heaven." (Matthew 7:15–21 ESV)

This teaching is applicable in all areas of life, but especially in terms of spiritual leadership. The qualifications of elders and deacons in the pastoral epistles reflect the need for leaders to be vetted by the outcome of their families.

> Therefore an overseer must be above reproach, the husband of one wife, sober-minded, self-controlled, respectable, hospitable, able to teach, not a drunkard, not violent but gentle, not quarrelsome, not a lover of money. He must manage his own household well, with all dignity keeping his children submissive, for if someone does not know how to manage his own household, how will he care for God's church?...
> Let deacons each be the husband of one wife, managing their children and their own households well. (1 Timothy 3:2–5, 12 ESV)

> Appoint elders in every town as I directed you—if anyone is above reproach, the husband of one wife, and his children are believers and not open to the

charge of debauchery or insubordination. (Titus 1:5–6 ESV)

Caring for one's family and raising them to faith was one indicator that what went on at home was the same as one's public expression of faith.

There are no simple answers to the question of how to raise faithful Christians. But all would agree that a major hindrance to spiritual parenting would be hypocrisy at home, or the lack of what we have defined here as integrity. Our children would stumble seeing us play the hypocrite. This is not about being perfect disciples, but it is about us being real. One of the best lessons we teach our children is as an example of repentance. It is a lesson they must learn to be saved and to have lasting relationships with others as well.

Fifth, the home needs to be filled with love, joy, respect, and affection. In all spiritual leadership, there must be the ability to connect to those we lead. In the family, love and affection are paramount.

· Chapter Fifteen ·

Keeping the Standards High

We Are Soldiers in the Army
We are soldiers in the army.
We have to fight although we have to cry.
We've got to hold up the bloodstained banner.
We've got to hold it up until we die!

In Roman warfare, medieval warfare, and nineteenth century warfare, the standard-bearer had an important role on the battlefield. The standard-bearer acted as an indicator of where the position of a military unit was. The standard was a bright and colorful flag acting as a strong visual beacon to surrounding soldiers. Soldiers were typically ordered to follow and stay close to the standard or flag in order to maintain unit cohesion, and for a single commander to easily position his troops by only positioning his standard-bearer, typically with the aid of musical cues or loud verbal commands. It was an honorable position carrying a considerable risk, as a standard-bearer would be a major target for the opposing side's troops seeking to capture the standard or pull it down. In the Roman military, the person carrying the standard was called the signifer.

"Banner" and "standard" militarily are synonyms. During a battle, in the midst of all the smoke and dust of warfare, it was difficult to know where the battle line was. So it was someone's job to be the standard bearer so that the troops and officers could coordinate their efforts effectively. Without this, confusion would reign. The opposing side tried to eliminate those holding the standards high to increase that confusion. They were easy targets as they just stood on that battle line without seeking cover. It would take bravery and duty to stand so that you could be seen clearly, rather than hiding in the crowd, the masses, the mob.

As the metaphor of battle is used figuratively in the New Testament and literally in the Old Testament, one sees the same attack on those who stand firm. It seems to fit well with the Apostle Paul's usage as he described the spiritual armor we are meant to be clothed in for our spiritual warfare. He highlights the need to stand.

> Put on the whole armor of God, that you may be able to stand against the schemes of the devil. For we do not wrestle against flesh and blood, but against the rulers, against the authorities, against the cosmic powers over this present darkness, against the spiritual forces of evil in the heavenly places. Therefore take up the whole armor of God, that you may be able to withstand in the evil day, and having done all, to stand firm. (Ephesians 6.11–13)

Unless spiritual leaders take a stand and stand firm, the battle line is confused. Not surprisingly, people are confused about who the real enemy is, and the united front is lost. Often this results in collateral damage to our own people rather than being united against our real enemy. This is played out time and time again in the church.

To stand when others run or hide is the call to all who are in spiritual leadership positions. David's mighty men are best described as this kind of men. When others ran, they stood!

> And next to him was Shammah, the son of Agee the Hararite. The Philistines gathered together at Lehi, where there was a plot of ground full of lentils, and the men fled from the Philistines. But he took his stand in

the midst of the plot and defended it and struck down the Philistines, and the LORD worked a great victory. (2 Samuel 23:11–12 ESV)

What are the standards that biblically should be held up and firmly adhered to?

First, that the Scriptures are our standard. We don't go beyond what is written: "I have applied all these things to myself and Apollos for your benefit, brothers, that you may learn by us not to go beyond what is written, that none of you may be puffed up in favor of one against another" (1 Corinthians 4:6 ESV). To go beyond our standard (our battle line), which is the word of God, is to arrogantly (being puffed up) think we know best and know what the real issues are. We get sidetracked by our culture and misdirected away from Scripture as our standard.

Second, our mission is to seek and save the lost:

"For the Son of Man came to seek and to save the lost." Luke 19:10

Here is a trustworthy saying that deserves full acceptance: Christ Jesus came into the world to save sinners—of whom I am the worst. (1 Timothy 1:15)

Most estimates of the number of Christians at the end of the first century are around ten thousand. By the end of the second century, the estimates are a hundred thousand. These numbers don't register with our reading of the Jerusalem church in Acts, the only church where numbers were ever mentioned in the New Testament.

But what happened after the explosion of the church in Jerusalem following the martyrdom of Stephen, a church numbering 5,000 men, not counting women and children? When the new disciples were scattered and returned to their homes throughout the diaspora, would they have followed a similar pattern we see now when new Christians move to an area without a church or New Testament or cell phone? What impact did the false teachers, the Judaizers, Docetists, gnostics and many others have on many who became disciples? How many converts were lost?

I say all this so that, though we should care deeply about bearing much fruit, fruit that will last, we should not lose our efforts to save as many as possible. And part of the process of finding the good soil implies that most who hear the message will not survive, as in the parable of the four soils.

If many left the first century church, there were still 10,000 who hadn't. By the end of the second century there would be 100,000. By the end of the third century there would be an estimated five or six million.

So again, keep standing on our mission.

Third, we must keep our standards of righteousness high.

> And many false prophets will arise and lead many astray. And because lawlessness will be increased, the love of many will grow cold.
> But the one who endures to the end will be saved. And this gospel of the kingdom will be proclaimed throughout the whole world as a testimony to all nations, and then the end will come. (Matthew 24:11–13 ESV)

In modern Christianity, tolerance has been added to the fruits of the Holy Spirit. Unfortunately, it is not in the list in Galatians 5:22. Jesus says that as lawlessness (NIV: wickedness) increases, the love of many will grow cold. I believe he is talking about those in the church, not outside the church.

Issues of purity, marriage, and greed are just a few examples of this increase in lawlessness.

If you wonder why the commitment and love of many in the church seems to have gone off the boil to slowly cooling to room temperature, is it because the standards of righteousness have been lowered? When was the last time you were in a discipleship group or accountability group? When was the last time your righteousness was challenged? Hebrews 3:12 admonishes us to "see to it, brothers and sisters, that none of you has a sinful, unbelieving heart that turns away from the living God."

Akoúō ("to hear") is virtually the only Greek word for hearing, but there are several words for seeing. Here in Hebrews 3, *blépō,* one of the various words in Greek for seeing, means "to see" with a stronger emphasis on the function of the eye. It is to use our eyes to look closely. It is not a suggestion in this text, but a command in the imperative tense. This is not about being spiritual police officers, but it is about not blurring what sin really is or means. It is a command to the brothers and sisters to keep our standards high lest the love of many in our fellowship grow cold.

What standards do we uphold as leaders? To back down leaves God's people fighting with each other rather than waging the spiritual battle we are meant to be engaged in as disciples of Jesus.

As so many spiritual songs and hymns remind us, our standard and banner is Jesus. Let us unashamedly raise it high to be seen by all!

· Chapter Sixteen ·

Epilogue: Broad Platform of Leadership

Remember your leaders, those who spoke the word of God to you. Consider the outcome of their way of life and imitate their faith. Jesus Christ is the same yesterday and today and forever. (Hebrews 13:7–8)

Obey your leaders and submit to them, for they are keeping watch over your souls, as those who will have to give an account. Let them do this with joy and not with groaning, for that would be of no advantage to you. (Hebrews 13:17 ESV)

And what you have heard from me in the presence of many witnesses entrust to faithful men, who will be able to teach others also. (2 Timothy 2:2 ESV)

The writer of Hebrews and the Apostle Paul deliberately use the plural for leaders, not the singular. This does not undermine the need for a lead evangelist, but it does say that leadership should have a broad platform. Both the Old Testament and New Testament teach and practice this in regard to leadership. Elders, advisers, prophets, kings, evangelists, and deacons are some of the roles mentioned in the Scriptures.

Jesus chose twelve apostles, and Paul had a group of men and women that he shared responsibilities with for those churches that he served and oversaw.

So one role of proper spiritual leadership is making sure one is involved in broadening the platform of leaders. There are commands to continue this process for the health of God's church. Titus is to make sure he finishes his assignment in Crete: "This is why I left you in Crete, so that you might put what remained into order, and appoint elders in every town as I directed you" (Titus 1:5 ESV).

The writer of Hebrews 3:12-13 gives the charge to "take care, brothers, lest there be in any of you an evil, unbelieving heart, leading you to fall away from the living God. But exhort one another every day, as long as it is called 'today,' that none of you may be hardened by the deceitfulness of sin" (ESV). This is especially true when one is leading. There is something very common in leadership personalities that is prone to resist raising up other leaders if it means empowering those leaders. It is seen so clearly in a world where dictators exist, leading to a paranoia of rivals who might endanger their positions. But this can be seen in God's people as well. The kings of Israel often resisted and even persecuted any prophet or adviser who challenged their performance. It is seen in many church leaders who after many years still control their little empire. Instead of being convicted that after twenty-plus years no elders have been appointed, they defend their position with excuses rather than owning their incompetence. Paul charges us all to have a sober judgment of our own competence.

The raising up of leaders will organically grow the church. Raising up disciples who can make disciples will determine growth. If the growth of the church is the same each year, then the same number of people who can convert others to Christ usually is static. The church is not multiplying but adding those who know Christ. But in raising the number of those who can make other disciples, then it changes from addition to multiplication.

Here are some practical suggestions.

First, have a leadership training program (LTP) where disciples are asked to join rather than it being an open invitation. It should meet monthly, with lessons given on spiritual leadership. This creates a group of likeminded disciples who want to be used by God in whatever way he chooses. This atmosphere can inspire one another to greater service. It is no coincidence that world records are broken at the Olympics. There is an atmosphere that brings out excellence.

Second, always be expanding to regions where there are more opportunities for people to exercise leadership while still remaining in a training position. This follows growth, as the midweeks and some Sunday services can be split to better reach our larger metropolitan areas and give members a more local feel to their ministries. If you are fearful of letting go of control and influence, then you might need to remind yourself whose church it really is and that part of your job description is to entrust to faithful men and women who will equip others. If none are raising up, then there is a need to adjust your service and raise your delegating practices.

Third, be willing to take risks. There is a danger of promoting leadership to those not ready for it at their stage of development, the premature "laying on of hands." But there is also a danger of being too faithless and more concerned with failures than success. There seems to be a faithlessness that has permeated church cultures worldwide.

Fourth, delegation is part of Timothy's charge in 2 Timothy 4:5: "As for you, always be sober-minded, endure suffering, do the work of an evangelist, fulfill your ministry" (ESV). "Fulfill" is the Greek word *plērophoréō*. This late compound means "to bring to fullness" in such senses as "to fulfill or complete" (TDNT). It is our job to make sure we replicate ourselves to faithful disciples to continue to build God's kingdom. Moses needed input from his father-in-law to delegate to others so that God's people would be better cared for as his sheep (Exodus 18).

Fifth, biblical authority is given to both evangelists and elders. There is not meant to be a conflict over who is in charge. We need to see ourselves as all building God's house, and in the building process there are different roles. We are not checks and balances on each other in a negative sense. We are all checks and balances with each other as disciples of Christ. We need to see ourselves as co-builders.

Sixth, have discipleship groups where you lead the process of openness so that you can get local discipling from those who know you best and who see your leadership in practice. It is like studying about sin with someone and leading the study by re-acting to sin lists in Scripture with examples from your own life, which encourages the one you are teaching to be open as well. It is always humbling and refreshing in a painfully good way. So in discipleship groups, lead first and foremost by example and transparency to train everyone else to always be open and transparent.

Seventh, be aware that "autonomy" is not a biblical word or concept. "Autonomy" is from two Greek words, *autos:* self, and *nomos:* govern, rule; i.e., self-rule or self-government. Where is this concept taught in the New Testament? Self-rule is not compatible with lordship. I grew up in a church that stressed autonomy as a biblical church model. There was little outside influence or cooperation. It was notable that the average member also applied it to their own life. No one had the right to look deeply into another's life. The result did not produce the unity that Paul expected "that you be united in the same mind and the same judgment" (1 Corinthians 1:10 ESV). So it is important to get outside influence to reduce dysfunction. Local decision-making and being open to outside advice are compatible. There will always be conflicts locally that need some objective outside input. If it is true of our marriages, it is true for our churches.

Chapter Seventeen

Partnership in Leading

Teresa Fontenot

> Then the LORD God said, "It is not good that the man should be alone; I will make him a helper fit for him." (Genesis 2:18 ESV)

The first negative thing that God says about his creation is that man should not be alone. God then created woman, and humanity became two separate, equal, and unique parts. Eve was both essential and invaluable to the world God had created. Now all was good and right in the world.

The *Ezer*

But what does it mean to be the helper? On the surface, it doesn't sound very impressive.

"Helper" comes from the Hebrew word *ezer*. *Ezer* appears twenty-one times in the Old Testament. Twice in Genesis it describes the woman. But the majority of references, sixteen, refer to God, or Yahweh, as the helper of his people, and the remaining three references appear in the books of the prophets, who use it to refer to military aid. The *ezer*, in every case, is a very strong helper.

Together both male and female are created in God's image, therefore the qualities of Yahweh are exemplified in both, the quality of God's strength in helping his people being dominant in the female. She was created for relationship, support, and strength. The *ezer* will be the one to come alongside and fight to make known the image of God to his creation. The authority to portray this image is given to the male (later known as Adam), but he cannot do it alone. God has provided the perfect solution, a female counterpart. She will be his greatest influencer in life on earth. As free will is given to all humanity, the result will be both good and bad, and all are held responsible.

The Disciple

There is, of course, no distinction when it comes to following and obeying God as the ultimate leader and authority in all our lives. We are called to have faith in him, to seek his will and obey his commands. There is no substitute for this relationship. Any substitution is considered idolatry and violates the first commandment Yahweh handed down to Moses. Therefore, our first loyalty and devotion are always in our discipleship to God. Jesus cleared up any confusion about this point when he corrected Martha for wanting her sister Mary to pull herself away from the conversation with Jesus and get busy serving their guests. Luke says, "And she had a sister called Mary, who sat at the Lord's feet and listened to his teaching" (Luke 10:39 ESV). The terminology of "sitting at the feet" of someone is used in reference to the discipling relationship of a disciple to the rabbi. Mary had taken this posture with Jesus, and he explains to her sister that Mary has made the best choice. He defends her right to become his disciple alongside the men he was training. The priority for all humans is to "seek first the kingdom of God and his righteousness" (Matthew 6:33 ESV).

The Leader

Throughout biblical history women have fulfilled roles of leadership. In the Old Testament we have the books of Ruth and Esther along with the story of Deborah the judge and prophetess and Jael, the wife of Heber, as prime examples. There are also women such as Miriam the prophetess and Rahab the prostitute, as well as others named and unnamed.

In the New Testament we have women such as Mary, Jesus'

mother, Mary Magdalene, and others in their discipleship group supporting Jesus' ministry. The woman at the well, who led her whole village to investigate this man Jesus, is an example. There is Lydia leading women in worship, and Priscilla supporting Paul alongside her husband, Aquila, just to name a few.

Women played key roles in the beginning of Jesus' life, and they were also there at his death and his resurrection. They were eyewitnesses of key events that would change history. Although Jesus did not choose women to be apostles, he taught them intimately and publicly without distinction. He admonished them, but never rebuked a woman. He even waited for a woman to arrive to witness the resurrection and then carry that good news to the apostles. But it would be Peter who would stand and proclaim the good news at Pentecost. In spiritual leadership, there are clear roles given; just as God, Jesus, and the Holy Spirit differ in their roles, men and women have different roles to fulfill. It is essential for a healthy church that these distinct roles are fulfilled to proclaim the full image of God. If we were exactly the same, one of us would be redundant. Women are designed to lead in submission to men, but never less than men. Although we are all called to submit to one another and respect one another, this is a primary role to be exemplified by women, and especially those in leadership. Miriam learned this the hard way.

Women, alongside men, are given the gift of spiritual leadership. As has already been mentioned, there were women who prophesied. Acts 21:7-9 refers to Philip's four daughters who prophesied. This was fulfilling the scripture that Peter preached in Acts 2:17. Other women who prophesied include Miriam (Exodus 15:20), Deborah (Judges 4:4), Huldah (2 Kings 22:14), Noadiah (Nehemiah 6:14), Isaiah's wife (Isaiah 8:3), and Anna (Luke 2:36-38). This was always to be done in submission to the leadership of the men in a respectful and orderly way, as Paul points out in 1 Corinthians 11:3-16. There is much more that can be discussed in Paul's instructions to the church in Corinth, but one thing is very clear, and that is the attitude of humility, submission, and respect when using our spiritual gifts to encourage the church.

Paul actively led alongside women in his ministry. He mentions them in several of his letters. In Philippians 4:2–3, Paul speaks of Euodia and Syntyche as women who "contended at my side in the cause of the gospel, along with Clement and the rest of my coworkers, whose names are in the book of life." I believe Paul valued the leadership and influence of women in his ministry. In Acts 16:13–15, Lydia persuaded him and his company to stay at her house. He was a frequent companion of Priscilla and Aquila as they made tents and spread the gospel together. Tentmaking was a time-consuming process, and they must have had many interesting conversations while they worked. Priscilla, whose name appears first five out of the seven times she and Aquila are mentioned in Scripture, would have exercised her influence on Paul as she was learning from him. Paul was interested in winning as many as possible, and of course, many of these would be women. I'm sure he valued input from godly women as they contended at his side. Paul often spoke, as he did earlier in his letter to the church in Philippi, of how the disciples should strive, contend, and labor together to have one mind for the sake of the gospel: "Only let your manner of life be worthy of the gospel of Christ, so that whether I come and see you or am absent, I may hear of you that you are standing firm in one spirit, with one mind striving side by side for the faith of the gospel" (Philippians 1:27 ESV).

In my experience, this cannot come about without much talking, listening, and understanding. But our unity of purpose, to make God known to a lost world, keeps us striving to achieve this "one mind," beyond our own opinions and biases.

So practically, how do we achieve this? I recently did a study on the phrase "fellow workers," which Paul uses most frequently to describe the women in his life. From this phrase we get the word "synergy" in English. This word is used thirteen times in the New Testament. "Synergy" is from the Greek prefix *syn-* meaning "together" and *ergon* meaning "work." This is the word Paul uses: "working together with."

What is the simple definition of synergy? It is "the combined power of a group of things when they are working together that is greater than the total power achieved by each working separately." Teamwork at its best results in a synergy that can be very productive. "Fellow worker" refers to someone who is a team player, who does not seek to run or control things on their own, nor serve for selfish or personal agendas.

First, I think our attitude is key. We must always keep the end goal in sight as we strive for unity with our fellow workers. It is "for the faith of the gospel" that we are contending. We want to follow our Lord in his purpose: "For the Son of Man came to seek and to save the lost" (Luke 19:10). With this as our ultimate goal, we can set aside our personal feelings and agendas and create synergy. Of course, this is much more easily said than done. Keeping an attitude of humility and "seeking first his kingdom and his righteousness" is a daily and lifelong battle. But being clear that it is God I am pleasing first keeps me striving to crucify myself (and my self-interests) on a daily basis.

Second, I think we must have integrity, as has been discussed in an earlier chapter. Integrity means being honest and having strong moral principles based on Scripture. It's important that we love the truth and are willing to do what's right. There have been times when I have failed to have integrity and compromised to please others or my own self-interests. It never ended well, and of course, was not "a manner of life worthy of the gospel of Christ." It is far better to have security and integrity before God.

> Whoever walks in integrity walks securely,
> but whoever takes crooked paths will be
> found out. (Proverbs 10:9)

> In everything set them an example by doing what is good. In your teaching show integrity, seriousness and soundness of speech that cannot be condemned, so that those who oppose you may be ashamed because they have nothing bad to say about us. (Titus 2:7–8)

In our partnerships as we are leading, we must be honest and express our concerns, doubts, and frustrations, while keeping a respectful and supportive attitude. We will all stand before

God to give an account of what we have done here on earth. So, keeping a clear conscience is vital to integrity. Having integrity takes courage. One of my favorite examples of this in the Bible is Abigail. Her story is in 1 Samuel 25:1-44. In this story, Abigail is married to Nabal, who is a fool. He offends David and his men by not offering them hospitality for the kindness of their protection. David becomes angry and informs 400 of his men to strap on their swords and follow him to destroy Nabal and all his household. Abigail is told of this by her servants. She wastes no time. She gathers supplies for David and his men and heads out to bring about peace. She meets David in a ravine coming from the opposite direction, quickly dismounts, and bows before him with her face to the ground. She then delivers the longest speech made by any woman in the Hebrew Bible. In order to save her people, Abigail is confronting the "giant slayer." Her example in delivering this message is one that is an upward call for every woman to emulate.

- She quickly takes a posture of humility. (v. 23)

- She takes responsibility. (v. 24)

- She asks permission to speak, showing respect and giving David a chance to lower his guard.

- She speaks with candor and honesty. She knows her husband is a fool and has done a foolish thing. She doesn't make excuses or try to make the situation more palatable.

- Then, Abigail persuades David with faithful words. She portrays an absolute confidence in God and his plan.

- Abigail smoothly suggests the positive outcome to David and reminds him of his own values (v. 26).

- She presents his men with a present and then straightforwardly asks for forgiveness. (vv. 27-28)

- She emphasizes her positive view of David's character (vv. 28-29) and appeals to him to identify with those he intended to kill.

- She reminds him of his past victories due to his faith in God and of the future life God has promised him. (vv. 30–31). He would not want to do something that he would later regret.

Abigail brought about peace with an irate king who was on his way to war. Emotions were running high, but she stayed calm, focused, and faithful to the end that she knew God desired for everyone. She did all of this without informing her husband, who was known by all to be a fool. Abigail absolutely trusted God and his goodness in every area of her life.

Abigail is one of the great women influencers in the Bible. Influence travels through relationships and wins the heart and soul of another person through their character. Abigail found a kindred spirit in David and was wise enough to communicate their common hope in God through humility and grace. She inspired him to be the leader that God had anointed him to be and followed "a man after God's own heart."

Abigail never stepped out of her role of submission as a woman, a servant, and a wife, yet she changed history and the life of a king destined for greatness—all because she had the courage to stand with God. She proved herself to be a true daughter of Sarah as described in 1 Peter 3:6b "You are her daughters if you do what is right and do not give way to fear."

Integrity means we are sincere and forthright without compromising, but not stubborn or opinionated.

Abigail put the needs of others above her own and did what was righteous before God. As a result, God dealt with her husband Nabal, and she became David's wife. "A gracious woman gets honor" (Proverbs 11:16a ESV).

A basic human need is respect, and to form a great partnership, it is essential.

Treating someone with respect means:
- showing regard for their abilities and worth
- valuing their feelings and their views, even if you don't

necessarily agree with them

- accepting them on an equal basis and giving them the same consideration you would expect for yourself (*Psychology Today*)

In a godly marriage, the woman is particularly given the charge of having respect for her husband. "However, each one of you also must love his wife as he loves himself, and the wife must respect her husband" (Ephesians 5:33).

Although our partners in leadership are not always our husbands, I think that characterizing respect in that relationship brings the best godly example for the women to follow. Abigail showed great respect for David as a leader and a man of God, even when she disagreed with him. Respect is shown in our body language, tone of voice, and willingness to listen and understand the other person's point of view.

Abigail was able to hold David in such high regard, even in one of his most ungodly moments, because of her faith in God. We can give respect and even submit when we need to only if we believe God is guiding the outcome. Abigail's faith was tested in this encounter, but she reminded David of the certainty we have when we fight the Lord's battles. In my experience, it takes a great deal of faith to believe in God's sovereignty, especially in heightened moments of conflict. My sinful instincts are to either run from the fight or to lash out in anger, and neither brings about the godly respect God desires.

> My dear brothers and sisters, take note of this: Everyone should be quick to listen, slow to speak and slow to become angry, because human anger does not produce the righteousness that God desires. (James 1:19–20)

These verses have become my mantra. I have needed to memorize them and quote them frequently to myself.

· Chapter Eighteen ·

Ezers in Action

Teresa Fontenot

What does it look like to be that strong, warrior helper that God created you to be? Here are a few practicals that may help.

1. **Get Rid of Competitiveness.** We were all created uniquely to complete the ministry God has entrusted us with. We are not "running a race," but "building a house." A race is an individual effort, but building a house (or a kingdom in this case) takes many people with different skills to complete. We are warned of the dangers of selfish ambition in Philippians and James. When it becomes about me, it is no longer honoring Christ, who emptied himself for others. There should not be a competition between the men's and women's ministries. We each should be giving our best, using all our gifts and continuing to grow to become even more fruitful. There is no race if there is no competition. The Holy Spirit is not a competitive spirit.

2. **Be a Servant.** Throughout the Bible the term "serve" (servant, service, serving) is used hundreds of times. It is a quality that marks every godly person. Jesus exemplified it: "For even the Son of Man came not to be served but to serve, and to give his life as a ransom for many" (Mark 10:45 ESV). The only time he used the

word "example" of himself was when he washed the apostles' feet.

> "If I then, your Lord and Teacher, have washed your feet, you also ought to wash one another's feet. For I have given you an example, that you also should do just as I have done to you. Truly, truly, I say to you, a servant is not greater than his master, nor is a messenger greater than the one who sent him. If you know these things, blessed are you if you do them." (John 13:14–17 ESV)

Serving is the norm for a leader. Look for and anticipate needs. Then find solutions to meet them. Serve your leaders and coleader. Jesus had a band of women around him who looked for ways to meet his needs. Hospitality was a particular responsibility of women, and they made sure that the physical needs of Jesus and the apostles were taken care of. Shepherds are called to be "eager to serve" in 1 Peter 5:2b. Looking for ways to serve takes our thoughts away from ourselves and onto others, overcoming the temptation to be insecure. Look for needs throughout the fellowship. Don't forget to look in the corners of the room.

3. **Communication Is More Than the Words You Say.** Communication is important for any healthy working relationship. You must keep your partner informed of situations and events in the ministry. It is better to overcommunicate and then be informed of what is needed than to not communicate enough and leave the other person guessing. When we must fill in the blanks, we often get it wrong. So much communication these days is sent in messages of various forms. We are all aware of how these messages can be misinterpreted.

The person does not see your face or hear the humor you intended. Paul and John sent messages, but they expressed their longing to speak "face to face." There is no substitute for talking together in the same room. Misunderstandings are more easily explained, and forgiveness is more freely given when we look into each other's eyes. Our communication with a male leadership partner is particularly important because it sets the tone for others to follow: Does she speak to him respectfully? Does she have confidence in him, giving him the benefit of the doubt? Does she seem fearful of him or resentful toward him? Is she dismissive, not taking him seriously? Is she authoritative and dominant in how she speaks? Maybe a bit "bossy"? Is she frustrated? Does she leave the conversation upset and unresolved? I understand all these possibilities; they are human, but others will follow our lead. Our level of respect in communication will be noted by others and imitated, even without knowing it. Don't worry if you have gotten it wrong. You can always apologize, and others will know it was wrong, and you can reset.

The problem I have experienced many times is not the actual words that are spoken, but the tone, the body language, and the manner in which they are delivered. I have often been thinking more of the content and the meaning of my words than the packaging or delivery process. How many times have you heard someone say, "That's not what I meant!"? It is usually because the delivery did not match the meaning. Unfortunately, we cannot hear what it is like to be on the other end of our communiqué, so we must be humble and ask, "How did I come across to you?" We often don't know that we are frustrated, angry, or dismissive in our tone until someone is kind enough to inform us. Don't just assume that someone got your meaning; ask what they heard. And we must be humble enough to ask how to communicate more effectively in future. Since the whole gospel message is brought through words, no wonder Jesus said that we will be judged for every careless one. We can always improve in this area. It is all the more important when we are speaking to people of different cultures and backgrounds.

Another form of communication is our faces and our bodies. What are they doing? Do I have my arms crossed, am I sitting back, pointing a finger, shifting from foot to foot? Am I looking away, avoiding eye contact? Am I frowning, furrowing my brow, sighing? All these ways we look communicate something to our listener. Again, BE HUMBLE and GET INPUT! None of us knows how we seem to others. I asked a sister years ago why everyone was asking me if I was OK. She told me that I have a mouth that turns down when I'm just relaxed, so it looks like I'm unhappy. I was tempted to complain to the Potter for how he had formed my mouth, but instead I made an effort from then on to smile as much as possible to let people know I was happy. People are observant. Be aware of your attitudes before you speak. They will come through in what you say. Deal with your heart and wait until your emotions have calmed before speaking. I have learned that people don't remember what you said, but they remember how you made them feel. Develop a caring and honest relationship with your partner, so that things can be brought up in a gracious and helpful way. Settle matters quickly between the two of you, as the Bible instructs. "Be completely humble and gentle; be patient, bearing with one another in love. Make every effort to keep the unity of the Spirit through the bond of peace" (Ephesians 4:2–3).

4. **Train Women to Lead.** In order to train women for leadership, they must be given opportunities to lead.

We need people who can lead on all levels of service in the church. There is always a need for more Bible discussion group leaders. In order for the women to be trained, they should be given responsibility for leading groups and learning to take responsibility for the growth of their members. The women do not have as many opportunities to speak, so we need to create those opportunities by having women's events where the women can speak directly to the needs of the women. Through the years, we have had women's Bible talks, Women's Days (for the purpose of evangelism), Women of the Word (to preach about a particular woman of the Bible or a biblical topic particularly relevant to women, encouraging the Christians and their friends), women's biblical series, sharing in communion, or teaching alongside the men in various ministries. We are not called to step in front of the men nor to teach the men publicly on our own, but we should teach the women at every opportunity. Teaching a woman how to become a Christian is one of the greatest skills we can ever learn. There are many steps to help someone understand what it means to make Jesus Lord of their lives. We need many opportunities to increase our effectiveness in this area. Be persuasive with your male counterpart when it comes to facilitate this training for the women. Paul instructed in Titus 2:3-5 that Titus was to teach the older women, and they were to teach the younger women "what is good." He then includes very practical and specific needs for the women's ministry. This is a good guideline and example to us, that women need to be teaching women.

5. **Don't Run From the Fight.** Conflict...just the word it-self can bring on stress. Do you feel yourself tensing up at this topic? I don't think that is unusual or ab-normal. If we really enjoyed conflict, then we wouldn't

make very good leaders. But nevertheless, life is conflict! There is no healthy life without it. We're told that persevering through the hard times is what builds our character, and no fruit comes without pruning. There will be pain. There will be conflict, but the promise is more fruitfulness as a result. We all have times when we run from conflict and other times when we run toward it, depending on the situation and our attitude at the time. Women are hardwired for fear. Fear is usually our default drive and comes with little effort. But 1 John 4:18 tells us that *there is no fear in love.* Fear and love repel each other, just as when like poles of two magnets are brought together and they push apart. So the opposite of love is not hate, but fear. When we are fearful, we are not loving. We cannot bridge the gap. We cannot make peace. I am more motivated to overcome fear when I decide to be more loving. Fear can be powerful, but love is more so. Follow biblical guidelines when dealing with conflict. God always knows how humans can attain peace. Go with love, humility, and courage—all courtesy of the Holy Spirit God placed within you. Things will not always turn out the way we desire, or even the way God desires, but we do have an enemy to fight, and he is not your brother or sister. Warfare, even spiritual warfare, is difficult and dangerous, but it is what *ezers* were created for. Then again, sometimes we need to back away and leave it to the men who are the stronger vessels. We can be the support.

Books at www.ipibooks.com

Books at www.ipibooks.com

Books at www.ipibooks.com

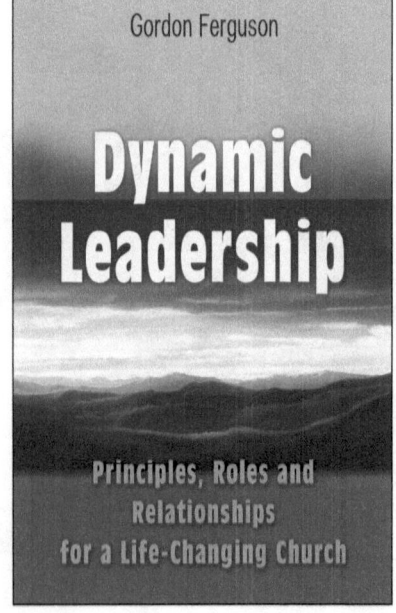

Books at www.ipibooks.com

Books for Christian Growth from Illumination Publishers

Apologetics

Compelling Evidence for God and the Bible—Truth in an Age of Doubt, by Douglas Jacoby.
Field Manual for Christian Apologetics, by John M. Oakes.
Is There A God—Questions and Answers about Science and the Bible, by John M. Oakes.
Mormonism—What Do the Evidence and Testimony Reveal?, by John M. Oakes.
Reasons For Belief-A Handbook of Christian Evidence, by John M. Oakes.
That You May Believe—Reflections on Science and Jesus, by John Oakes/David Eastman.
The Resurrection: A Historical Analysis, by C. Foster Stanback.
When God Is Silent—The Problem of Human Suffering, by Douglas Jacoby.

Bible Basics

A Disciple's Handbook—Third Edition, Tom A. Jones, Editor.
A Quick Overview of the Bible, by Douglas Jacoby.
Be Still, My Soul—A Practical Guide to a Deeper Relationship with God, by Sam Laing.
From Shadow to Reality—Relationship of the Old & New Testament, by John M. Oakes.
Getting the Most from the Bible, Second Edition, by G. Steve Kinnard.
Letters to New Disciples—Practical Advice for New Followers of Jesus, by Tom A. Jones.
The Baptized Life—The Lifelong Meaning of Immersion into Christ, by Tom A. Jones.
The Lion Never Sleeps—Preparing Those You Love for Satans Attacks, by Mike Taliaferro.
The New Christian's Field Guide, Joseph Dindinger, Editor.
Thirty Days at the Foot of the Cross, Tom and Sheila Jones, Editors.

Christian Living

According to Your Faith—The Awesome Power of Belief in God, by Richard Alawaye.
But What About Your Anger—A Biblical Guide to Managing Your Anger, by Lee Boger.
Caring Beyond the Margins—Understanding Homosexuality, by Guy Hammond.
Free Your Mind—40 Days to Greater Peace, Hope, and Joy, by Sam Laing.
Golden Rule Membership—What God Expects of Every Disciple, by John M. Oakes.
How to Defeat Temptation in Under 60 Seconds, by Guy Hammond.
Jesus and the Poor—Embracing the Ministry of Jesus, by G. Steve Kinnard.
How to Be a Missionary in Your Hometown, by Joel Nagel.
Jesus the Master Teacher—Transforming Our Hearts, by Jeanie Shaw
Like a Tree Planted by Streams of Water—Personal Spiritual Growth, G. Steve Kinnard.
Love One Another—Importance & Power of Christian Relationships, by Gordon Ferguson.
My Roller Coaster Ride with God and Cancer, by Gordon Ferguson.
One Another—Transformational Relationships, by Tom A. Jones and Steve Brown.
Prepared to Answer—Restoring Truth in An Age of Relativism, by Gordon Ferguson.
Repentance—A Cosmic Shift of Mind & Heart, by Edward J. Anton.
Strong in the Grace—Reclaiming the Heart of the Gospel, by Tom A. Jones.
The Guilty Soul's Guide to Grace—Freedom in Christ, by Sam Laing.
The Power of Discipling, by Gordon Ferguson.
The Prideful Soul's Guide to Humility, by Tom A. Jones and Michael Fontenot.
The Way of the Heart—Spiritual Living in a Legalistic World, by G. Steve Kinnard.
The Way of the Heart of Jesus—Prayer, Fasting, Bible Study, by G. Steve Kinnard.
Till the Nets Are Full—An Evangelism Handbook for the 21st Century, by Douglas Jacoby.
Walking the Way of the Heart—Lessons for Spiritual Living, by G. Steve Kinnard.
When God is Silent—The Problem of Human Suffering, by Douglas Jacoby.
Values and Habits of Spiritual Growth, by Bryan Gray.

All Available at www.ipibooks.com

Deeper Study

A Women's Ministry Handbook, by Jennifer Lambert and Kay McKean.
After The Storm—Hope & Healing From Ezra—Nehemiah, by Rolan Dia Monje.
Aliens and Strangers—The Life and Letters of Peter, by Brett Kreider.
Crossing the Line: Culture, Race, and Kingdom, by Michael Burns.
Daniel—Prophet to the Nations, by John M. Oakes.
Exodus—Making Israel's Journey Your Own, by Rolan Dia Monje.
Exodus—Night of Redemption, by Douglas Jacoby.
Finish Strong—The Message of Haggai, Zechariah, and Malachi, by Rolan Dia Monje.
In Remembrance of Me—Understanding the Lord's Supper, by Andrew C. Fleming.
In the Middle of It!—Tools to Help Preteen and Young Teens, by Jeff Rorabaugh.
Into the Psalms—Verses for the Heart, Music for the Soul, by Rolan Dia Monje.
King Jesus—A Survey of the Life of Jesus the Messiah, by G. Steve Kinnard.
Jesus Unequaled—An Exposition of Colossians, by G. Steve Kinnard.
Letters from Jesus to the Seven Churches of Revelation, by Rolan Dia Monje
Mornings in Matthew, by Tammy Fleming.
Passport to the Land of Enough—Revised Edition, by Joel Nagel.
Prophets I—The Voices of Yahweh, by G. Steve Kinnard.
Prophets II—The Prophets of the Assyrian Period, by G. Steve Kinnard.
Prophets III—The Prophets of the Babylonian and Persion Periods, by G. Steve Kinnard.
Return to Sender—When There's Nowhere Left to God but Home, by Guy Hammond.
Romans—The Heart Set Free, by Gordon Ferguson.
Revelation Revealed—Keys to Unlocking the Mysteries of Revelation, by Gordon Ferguson.
Spiritual Leadership for Women, Jeanie Shaw, Editor.
Spiritual Leadership—Developing Qualities Worth Following, by Mike Fontenot.
The Call of the Wise—An Introduction and Index of Proverbs, by G. Steve Kinnard.
The Cross of the Savior—From the Perspective of Jesus..., by Mark Templer.
The Final Act—A Biblical Look at End-Time Prophecy, by G. Steve Kinnard.
The Gospel of Matthew—The Crowning of the King, by G. Steve Kinnard.
The Letters of James, Peter, John, Jude—Life to the Full, by Douglas Jacoby.
The Lion Has Roared—An Exposition of Amos, by Douglas Jacoby.
The Seven People Who Help You to Heaven, by Sam Laing.
The Spirit—Presense & Power, Sense & Nonsense, by Douglas Jacoby.
Thrive—Using Psalms to Help You Flourish, by Douglas Jacoby.
What Happens After We Die?, by Douglas Jacoby.
World Changers—The History of the Church in the Book of Acts, by Gordon Ferguson.

Marriage and Family

A Lifetime of Love—Building and Growing Your Marriage, by Al and Gloria Baird
Building Emotional Intimacy in Your Marriage, by Jeff and Florence Schachinger.
Hot and Holy—God's Plan for Exciting Sexual Intimacy in Marriage, by Sam Laing.
Faith and Finances, by Patrick Blair.
Friends & Lovers—Marriage as God Designed It, by Sam and Geri Laing.
Mighty Man of God—A Return to the Glory of Manhood, by Sam Laing.
Pure the Journey—A Radical Journey to a Pure Heart, by David and Robin Weidner.
Raising Awesome Kids—Being the Great Influence in Your Kids' Lives by Sam/Geri Laing.
Principle-Centered Parenting, by Douglas and Vicki Jacoby.
The Essential 8 Principles of a Growing Christian Marriage, by Sam and Geri Laing.
The Essential 8 Principles of a Strong Family, by Sam and Geri Laing.
Warrior—A Call to Every Man Everywhere, by Sam Laing.

Welcome
to the New

ILLUMINATION
PUBLISHERS
www.ipibooks.com

www.ipibooks.com

www.ingramcontent.com/pod-product-compliance
Lightning Source LLC
Chambersburg PA
CBHW021644120626
46545CB00002B/699